FRANK TEICHMANN (1937-2006) trained as an aircraft designer. He studied Egyptology and Classical Archaeology and was leader of the Anthroposophical Study Seminar in Stuttgart. He is the author of many books, including the series *Der Mensch und sein Tempel* (*Ägypten, Griechenland, Megalithkultur* and *Chartres*), *Der Gral im Osten, Die Kultur der Empfindungsseele, Die Kultur der Verstandesseele, Auferstehung im Denken, Die Ägyptischen Mysterien* and *Die Griechischen Mysterien.*

The Origins of the Anthroposophical Society in the Light of the Ancient Mysteries

Frank Teichmann

Translated from German by Paul King

TEMPLE LODGE

Temple Lodge Publishing Ltd.
Hillside House, The Square
Forest Row, RH18 5ES

www.templelodge.com

Published in English by Temple Lodge in 2020

Originally published in German under the title *Die Entstehung der Anthroposophischen Gesellschaft auf mysteriengeschichtlichem Hintergrund* by Verlag Freies Geistesleben, Stuttgart, in 2002

A CIP catalogue record for this book is available from the British Library

ISBN 978 1 912230 49 5

Cover by Morgan Creative featuring 'Druid Stone sketch' by Rudolf Steiner
Typeset by Symbiosys Technologies, Vishakapatnam, India
Printed and bound by 4Edge Ltd., Essex

Contents

Foreword

Under the surface and turmoil of everyday life, spiritual sources abide that have nourished the development of civilization and still contain the potential to inspire our personal and cultural lives. An impressive example of this is how Rudolf Steiner (1861-1925) used these sources and renewed their content in the process of developing his anthroposophy. Steiner often stressed their importance for the spiritualization of our culture, but hardly ever revealed how he himself worked with these sources or the crucial role they played in the development of anthroposophy. It is to the merit of Frank Teichmann (1937-2006) that he discovered this and traced it in such a detailed and convincing way. Teichmann's discovery was the fruit of a lifelong study of the ancient cultures of Europe and the Middle East combined with a profound knowledge of anthroposophy and the life of Rudolf Steiner. After being trained as an aeroplane engineer, Teichmann studied Egyptology and Classical Archaeology. From its foundation onwards, he was the longstanding leader of the Anthroposophical Study Seminar in Stuttgart. During those years he became a renowned lecturer and wrote numerous books on cultural history and the development of human consciousness. All these books, from his initial volumes on the Temples of Mankind to his final ones on the mysteries of Ancient Egypt and Greece, circle around the question of how culture and human consciousness are interrelated and have developed in relation to one another.

It was this specific background that enabled Frank Teichmann to recognize how Rudolf Steiner, in developing his anthroposophy, worked out of what he himself describes as the remains of the three major pre-Christian mystery-streams that nourished European culture: the Greek mysteries, the Egyptian mysteries and the mysteries of megalithic culture in northwestern Europe. In this process Steiner transformed their content in a Christian way and brought them to a new synthesis during the Christmas Conference of the Anthroposophical Society in 1923.

During its first development phase between around 1902-1908, still embedded within the Theosophical Society, anthroposophy was developed as a spiritual science in which rational thought, as initiated in Greek culture, was transformed into a living thought capable of acquiring spiritual knowledge.

From 1907 onwards, this spiritual content was brought to expression in both visual and musical arts. This culminated between 1913 and 1922 in the design for the first Goetheanum in Dornach as one of the most impressive examples of a Gesamtkunstwerk (a total work of art). For his artistic impulse, Rudolf Steiner connected to the last remnants of Egyptian spiritual life that once had focused on the question of how spirit and content can be embodied in matter and take visible shape.

It was only in 1923, during the difficult period that followed the First World War in Germany and after the first Goetheanum had burned down, that Rudolf Steiner came into contact with the remains of megalithic culture in Britain. Around that time megalithic culture was still considered to be rather primitive. But Steiner immediately recognized its specific spiritual content, for example in the relation of their monuments to the course of the sun and the cycle of the year. This encounter led to several series of lectures on the cycle of the year and the pre-Christian mysteries later that year, which prepared for and accompanied the Christmas Conference of 1923. During this conference the Anthroposophical Society was re-established and the Foundation Stone Meditation, which can be seen as a summary of the content of these three pre-Christian mystery streams, was given. As Teichmann points out, both were only possible because of Steiner's encounter with the remnants of north-western spirituality earlier that year.

The crucial role Rudolf Steiner's journeys to England and Wales played in the development of the Anthroposophical Society is little known, even among anthroposophists in Britain. It therefore is a great pleasure that the translation of his book now makes Frank Teichmann's detailed investigations into this subject available to the English-speaking world. In a world that is politically drifting apart, it is ever more important to be aware what contributions cultures and regions have made in the past and can potentially make in the future for the spiritualization of culture and the benefit of all humanity.

This book is not just relevant from a historical point of view or for a small group of anthroposophists. Reconnecting to our spiritual roots is essential for all of us. We are facing unprecedented ecological, social and cultural challenges for which new and unconventional answers have to be found. Paradoxically, connecting to the spiritual sources of ancient cultures can help us to find those answers. Not that they contain those answers, but because they have the ability to reawaken our own inner impulses. As Rudolf Steiner describes, we have all gone through numerous incarnations and carry the fruits of those incarnations, including the content of ancient mysteries, unconsciously in us. Between two incarnations, these fruits transform into will-impulses for a following life. Encountering the content or physical remains of ancient cultures can reawaken those impulses in us and make them conscious. Therefore this book is also a plea for what Steiner calls 'spirit recalling' in order to be able to meet the challenges of our time. What tremendous potential and impact this can have on social and cultural life is illustrated in an exemplary way in this book by the life and work of Rudolf Steiner.

The publication of this book would not have been possible without the generous support of dozens of individuals from all over the world. The initiative for it was born during an international meeting in the summer of 2018 at Ilkley (Yorkshire) and Penmaenmawr (Wales), the two major places where Steiner encountered the remains of megalithic culture. It was the first of a series of inspirational meetings organized by Sarri Tapales. She also devotedly coordinated the fundraising for the book that was generously supported by participants from England, Scotland, Ireland, the Netherlands, South Africa, Australia and the Philippines. Former students from Frank Teichmann in Germany and co-workers from his summer conferences in the Netherlands also joined the initiative, bridging national barriers in a shared impulse to support the renewal of spiritual life. We are very grateful to all those contributors who made this publication possible by their financial and moral support! Finally we want to thank the translator Paul King and the publisher Sevak Edward Gulbekian for their excellent work and good collaboration.

We hope this book will find its way to the hearts and minds of all those interested in the subject and that it will inspire them to deepen their insights and strengthen their will for the spiritualization of our culture.

Pieter van der Ree
June 2020

Preface

There is no clearer way of seeing what the Anthroposophical Society is and what it could be, than by looking at its founding impulses that shine out in the Christmas Conference of 1923. A great deal has already been written about this. Whether one was there and experienced it as the greatest event of one's life; whether one was so carried by the general [feeling of] spiritual upliftment that one understood only later what one had experienced as though in a dream; or whether we evaluate Rudolf Steiner's life differently today now that we can see it in its totality—different aspects are constantly emerging that shed new light on this event. In this book too it is a matter of presenting points of view that can make a contribution to the better understanding of what really happened at that time.

The Christmas Conference did not just appear out of nowhere, nor did it happen as the result merely of a decision on Rudolf Steiner's part. It was prepared for long beforehand. I don't mean by this the free preparation by Rudolf Steiner himself in accordance with his destiny. Rudolf Steiner was himself connected to a long stream of spiritual development in which he had already participated before his birth, indeed already in past spiritual streams. And it is out of the spirit that the anthroposophical movement and the Anthroposophical Society arose. This is clearly evident in Steiner's biography if we just pay attention to it. And that is what we propose to do here. I initially wanted to call the book The Christmas Conference in the Light of the History of the Mysteries, with reference to the great cycle of lectures on World History in the Light of Anthroposophy. I decided against this because it is perhaps simpler initially to look at the fundamental rays individually as they shine in one after the other, rather than where they all flow together from many sides.

Extending the material from there, I have only taken into account what was needed for the perspectives presented here, and left aside everything that would otherwise have to be looked at in a more external history of the anthroposophical movement. For example, the discussion and disagreement with the Theosophical Society, which spanned the whole period from 1907 to 1913, is barely mentioned because its contribution to the inner development of anthroposophy was fairly minimal. From the beginning, Rudolf Steiner taught and did what he held to be right, both at the beginning of his activity within the Theosophical Society and also during the phase of disagreement. The spiritual and artistic work was not impeded by this, and carried on uninterrupted. There was however a change in the emphasis of the work, on the one hand because this was an inner requirement, and on the other because new tasks came towards the anthroposophical movement from outside. But the most radical change occurred at the Christmas Conference itself, a change whose depths have not been fully fathomed even to this day.

The heated argument that flared up a few years ago over the statutes and constitution of the Anthroposophical Society have little to do with the view of the Christmas Conference presented in this book. At times it seems to me to be evasive action to avoid getting to grips with the spiritual challenges connected with the Christmas Conference when taken seriously. For statutes, of whatever kind they may be, can certainly never prevent an individual or a community of people from doing their own spiritual work!

This book is written for those who see anthroposophy as a significant aspect of their lives, and who wish to learn about its origins and how Rudolf Steiner brought it to the earth. Today, a hundred years after the beginning of his public work, the figure of this spiritual giant is gradually fading, and the less we know about him the more the impulse vanishes which was intended to become effective in our culture through him, those who worked with him, and his successors.

My own interest in the mysteries of pre-Christian times awoke a sense in me for mystery schools, so that I came to see, in the emergence of the anthroposophical movement, a recapitulation and renewal of the three types of mysteries. At first I just thought of the fundamental law of all human evolution, that when something new is to come into a culture, its past stages must first be repeated in abbreviated form, albeit unconsciously. As time went on, however, I became more and more astonished at how Rudolf Steiner had wanted to accomplish this consciously, also making a link with the last remnants reaching over to us from the period of the ancient mysteries. This gradually led to the discovery presented in this book: that the whole anthroposophical movement together with the Anthroposophical Society as it was re-founded at the Christmas Conference of 1923, was planned and prepared for in primordial times, and that these intentions were discovered by Rudolf Steiner and developed by him. All his deeds, no matter how original they may appear in the foreground, have a deep esoteric background that contains the entire spiritual history of humanity.

This permanent presence of spiritual history is significant for Rudolf Steiner whenever he wishes to act in a right and healing way. For this reason he refers again and again to past cultures, presents their spiritual sources, and also expects the members to have an interest in these connections. Each one of us carries around our own origin unconsciously, as though rolled up within ourself; in our day-consciousness we mostly know nothing of this, may even consider anyone who occupies themselves with history as living in times that are no longer relevant. Each one of us is a witness of these 'past' ages, and there is no better way, if we want to bring something new into our culture, than to become aware of our spiritual past. Only then, going beyond the everyday situation, can we participate in a higher development of culture. Giving attention and understanding to the spiritual impulses of past times is an urgent task especially for individuals interested in anthroposophy, because only through this can there emerge what we need today.

After the Christmas Conference, Rudolf Steiner revealed that every individual with an interest in anthroposophy took part before their descent to earth in a 'school' held by Michael for the souls who were spiritually prepared. They were taught there about all the past mysteries, 'Mystery centre after mystery centre was pursued'; but a foundation was also laid for the spiritualization of thinking, so that human beings learnt to value the means by which later, when on the earth, they could take hold again of the ancient spiritual content.

Finding anthroposophy and having an interest in it is something individuals can thank this school for. But taking hold of its content, practising thinking, feeling, and willing in order to be a co-worker in this work, is something the individual must decide on the earth itself.

As mentioned above, this book is written for anthroposophists, or at least for people who consider themselves to be such. For others, not involved in this way but still interested, the following pages might be a stimulus towards seeing anthroposophy in a broader historical context. Even the style of the book is chosen with this in mind. Rudolf Steiner's words are quoted without putting them into the context from which they are taken. This does not mean of course that it would not be possible to do so, but from the point of view chosen for the book, the sources are not necessary. I feel it necessary to state this at the beginning, otherwise people might be expecting something different. In addition I have made great efforts to be as succinct as possible. This was not always easy, particularly where the content of the ancient mysteries is concerned. I hope I have nevertheless remained intelligible.

Finally, as always, I wish to thank the people without whose engagement and interest the book could not have come about. Firstly I should like to mention the Iona-Stichting in Amsterdam, and above all Dolf van

Aalderen whose interest and involvement, which also took the form of a notable sum to sponsor the book, persuaded me to write on the theme. I should also like to thank my wife, as always, for being ready to correct my textual mistakes. I wish to thank Herr Neider and Herr Schneider for their collegial collaboration; and not least I should like to mention the Anthroposophical Society in Germany, in whose service I have put text to paper.

Frank Teichmann
Stuttgart, April 2002

Introduction

As contemporaries of the twentieth century it might seem remarkable to us, in a culture imbued with science and technology, and organized according to economic perspectives, to find a society that strives for a spiritualization of thinking and for a moral soul-life, that is concerned with understanding the being of the human individual from all sides, and which struggles for a deep understanding of the Christ event. Its members are interested in questions of destiny, life after death, and the reincarnation of the spirit, but also in the evolution of the cosmos, earth and human being, and the course of spiritual history. From an economic standpoint, none of these subjects is of any 'value'; they are of no use to technology or private profit; and yet, as everyone can see, our culture would quickly become impoverished without such questions. For, our actions, by which we advance civilization, depend to a high degree on the kind of thoughts we have concerning the human being and the cosmos. If we wish to work beneficially, then the goodness of our deeds will depend precisely on this, which is not something that stands obviously in the foreground or is dependent on technology. How a teacher teaches, for example, will be determined by how far they have developed the ability to work appropriately with the child's spiritual and intellectual stages of development. How an architect designs will depend on whether they have an awareness of the effect of forms on human soul-life, for without the architect intending it, these can be desolating. This applies similarly to the areas of medicine, agriculture, and social engagement—in short, in all areas that require moral actions. Even artists could take care over the effect their works have, for, depending on the artist's knowledge of the sources of their art, this can be very varied.

So how, we can ask, could a grouping of people like this, that is so contrary to the 'trend', actually come about? A group that has not come together for the sake of a clearly defined sphere of work, but which aims to be a practising society, to support the development of each individual, and hopes in this way to achieve something in our culture.

A group of people such as this could not have come about at all until the twentieth century. It is typical of our age. It would not have been thinkable in the nineteenth century if only because the process of individualization was not yet sufficiently advanced for there to be enough people for such a society. It requires inner confidence to go against general opinion.

We need only imagine, to take a drastic example, the situation of women in the last [the nineteenth] century, whose role was not yet seen as including emancipation. There were certainly a few individuals who had already attained intellectual independence but, with the exception of Goethe and his circle, they lived alone and without mutual support. And this living knowledge in certain individuals had not yet been outwardly applied in the different areas of life. Occasionally they taught at one or other of the universities, but the deeper knowledge they often had, and of which they were genuinely convinced, was kept to themselves and restricted to the intellectual penetration of phenomena as they presented themselves, and in extensive written work. Today the writings of those profound minds belong to what Rudolf Steiner called 'buried literature'.

If we ask why those sometimes great insights were not generally taken up, there is only one answer: because as a rule those in whom they originated did themselves not know how they came to them. Only very rarely were they at all conscious of the methodological difficulties, and more rarely still was there an individual who had themselves seen a path they could recommend whereby anyone else could have worked their way to similar findings. The later Immanuel Kant, and Johann Gottlieb Fichte, were such thinkers, and also Fichte's son, Immanuel Hermann Fichte, and possibly also Friedrich W J Schelling, but these are shining exceptions in an intellectual environment that was otherwise still working fairly unconsciously.

Rudolf Steiner was the first to recognize this dilemma and set about accomplishing what those great minds had not yet been able to accomplish. Right at the outset of his work he wrote *Grundlinien einer erkenntnistheorie der Goetheschen Weltanschaung mit besonderer Rücksicht auf Schiller* (1886) (Foundations of a theory of knowledge of the Goethean worldview with particular reference to Schiller), this was followed by *Wahrheit und Wissenschaft* (1892) (Truth and Knowledge/Science), and finally by *Die Philosophie der Freiheit* (1894) (The Philosophy of Freedom), whereby the methodological foundation was laid for all further 'spiritual science'. It was now possible to understand what the great idealists had wanted, but the requirement to lift ourselves up to the intellectual and spiritual heights in which they lived, was attained by only a few. Fundamentally, it is just as difficult today as it was then.

In 1979 The Club of Rome held a conference to discuss why 'progress' was proving so problematic. It found that 'people of our time, although highly developed in many respects, are not yet in a position to fully grasp the significance and consequences of their actions. Since the changes they make to their environment and their own living conditions are unconscious, the gap between humans and the real world is becoming ever greater. We call this gap the human dilemma, whose dimensions, although already extensive and dangerous, will almost inevitably increase.'[1]

These words of Aurelio Peccei only describe the old lack of knowledge in new words, but led to a number of institutions being tasked with investigating the cause of the lack. Surprisingly, their final report found human thinking to be the actual problem, since it is not able to follow movements or to encompass totalities. Accordingly, scientists call for a change in thinking and for a training of the capacities they call anticipation and integration, since it is on these that the future of humanity will depend.[2] Following on from these findings, the Club of Rome again commissioned certain institutions to investigate how this required thinking could be trained, but up to the present we have waited in vain for a result. No report has been forthcoming! This is hardly surprising, for when we burden institutions of natural science with spiritual tasks, they are by definition quite helpless, since hitherto such questions have not come within their remit.

It is interesting that these questions were resolved well over a hundred years ago, but are to be found in the 'buried literature' of those minds and thinkers who were aware of their methods. The zeitgeist of today is still calling for further development in our powers of thought as the prerequisite for a healthy future. Already in his notes on Goethe's scientific writings, and then later in many of his works, Rudolf Steiner gave exercises by which we can develop the desired thinking. It was just that the life situation of humanity was not so jeopardized at that time that people could immediately see what sort of future they actually had. People still thought they could regard the higher worlds as separate from the earthly situation; the fact that they belong together emerged only during the course of the anthroposophical movement's development.

It was also hard for Rudolf Steiner to find people open to such questions and who would be willing to get to grips with the tasks arising from them. He found them to begin with among a small group of 'theosophists' with whom, after shaking off the Eastern influences, he formed the Anthroposophical Society. When he took on the spiritual leadership of this in 1902, he was surely not certain what the consequences would be for him. Looking back, he divided the evolution of the Anthroposophical Society into three phases, each following the other sequentially, and each clearly distinct:

1. the scientific phase from 1902 to 1909,
2. the artistic phase from 1909 to 1916,
3. the phase of application in civilization from 1916 to 1923.

Each phase presupposes the preceding one whose activity, however, does not disappear but must be cultivated in a different way. Only once these three phases, each with its distinct character, had run their course, could Rudolf Steiner really found the Anthroposophical Society during the Christmas Conference of 1923. Many people felt that what happened there was the greatest event of their lives; but what really took place at the Christmas Conference is still the theme of engaged discussion.[3] That something new was beginning was already clear from the Foundation Stone verse which Steiner had worked on and developed for this event and which he hoped could indeed represent the inner foundation of every anthroposophist. This Foundation Stone directs the members towards a threefold 'practice...', corresponding to the three members of the Trinity, which is intended to give instruction related to a school with a threefold structure. After this event, these three separate areas no longer existed merely in juxtaposition or succession, but were intended to be one Society that had to take care of all three areas in relation to one another. What follows in this book is intended to show in specific detail what this means.

At the centre of anthroposophy lies the idea of development [or evolution], without which none of its content can actually be comprehended. This idea which, as the greatest achievement of German idealism, changed and dynamized the modern worldview, signifies for the individual the setting of a goal for oneself and then working towards its realization. Initially, what is important here, and what lies behind this striving, is to discover the Christ Being whose activity is the source of all endeavours towards perfection. To unite with Him, and to work in accordance with Christianity, is indeed the noblest task of every spiritually striving individual. Rudolf Steiner referred to this again and again, and even saw it as his task to make his contemporaries aware of it in order to ignite in them a striving for a deeper understanding of Christianity. The spiritual exercises given by Steiner during the course of the development of the anthroposophical schooling path, all serve the goal of discovering the Christ Being in our consciousness, and even learning to know it there. It is a path that is not based on dogmas or traditional faith, but which nevertheless takes seriously what is contained in the New Testament and seeks to understand it. Sooner or later every human being will attain what many who followed a path of practice have attained during the course of history, namely a conviction, through their own perception, of the continuing working of Christ.

Seen from what we now know, we can regard the background of Steiner's achievement—who developed anthroposophy and the

Anthroposophical Society, accompanied their progress, and developed them further right up to his death—to be this Christ experience. To this also belongs knowledge of the threefold structure of the ancient mysteries, which had the task, each from its own perspective on life, of leading its pupils to the central event of world evolution and making this comprehensible. It is wonderful to see how Steiner gradually masters the content of these mysteries once again, and receives from them the impulses he needed for the initial development of anthroposophy and then its further elaboration, and for the Anthroposophical Society. It is not the surface impressions of the nineteenth and twentieth centuries that lead to a spiritual science, but rather the mystery streams continuing to move in the depths, which were once cultivated in different centres but with a view to the future. It is there that we find the actual preparation for the renewal of a worldview based on the spirit.

So if we ask from what sources a movement like the anthroposophical movement could take shape in the twentieth century, we must point to a double impulse: On the one hand the 'spirit of the age' requires just such a movement, for the desired faculties of thinking cannot be developed without exercises. On the other hand, Steiner was able to connect to those underground currents that continue to work, and which made preparation for an understanding of the Christ mystery. It is part of the destiny of our times, as it were, that the faculties required from outside can be developed when we make a connection to the inner paths already prepared.

It is hoped that the following pages will show how this thesis can be understood. Those who take it to heart will perhaps better understand what is actually intended for the Anthroposophical Society precisely in our time, and why it is needed as an essential leaven in our culture. Its task, according to its original character, is to continue the great spiritual traditions of the Occident and to develop them further so that the decline of our present-day culture can be halted and turned around. Whether it manages this depends on how much commitment its members are able to muster. Its potential for development, however, is limitless!

The Theory of Evolution and its Consequences

Nothing comes into the world without preparation. This statement seems pretty self-evident, and yet it is worth pondering. Every beginning is initially inconspicuous and seminal, so that only sensitive and experienced people can get an inkling of what will emerge from it. More than anything, it is new ideas that remain the most hidden. Only a person moving in the same direction is in a position to hail and recognize the seminal energy in the work of someone else.

This is also the case with anthroposophy. It too comes into the world on silent feet to begin with, remaining unnoticed in a corner of cultural development, tolerated by humanist attitudes. And certainly no one suspected what it would become. Something very similar happened with the theory of evolution which arose at the turn of the nineteenth century and a hundred years later is still hotly contested. Even Haeckel finally wrote a book in 1905 which he called *Der Kampf um den Entwicklungsgedanken* (The battle over the theory of evolution).[4] This book also did not resolve the fundamental problems in any way, since the battle is still being waged today. Scientists have in the meantime certainly come to believe in evolution, but what this really means remains closed to them for the most part. It took a long time for it finally to become possible to think of the idea of evolution, and anyone who really thinks about it soon notices how difficult it is to encompass it in all its various and complicated ramifications.

This is not the place to go into the origins of the theory, but we do need a simplified outline of the basic idea in the form it was initially conceived in the first decade of the nineteenth century. At that time it had already developed so far as to be adequate for simple scientific phenomena. It proved more difficult however to apply it to the evolution of man. But let us look at the phenomenon of development and how it functions between a thing's essential *being* and its *appearance* [or manifestation], and facilitates a mediation of these two very different worlds with one another.

On the appearance side, we see how a thing continuously changes over the course of time, does not stay at any one point, and gradually undergoes transformation through various stages according to a system of laws. We can observe a plant, for example, how it pushes out the cotyledons from the seed, then spreads leaf after leaf along the stem

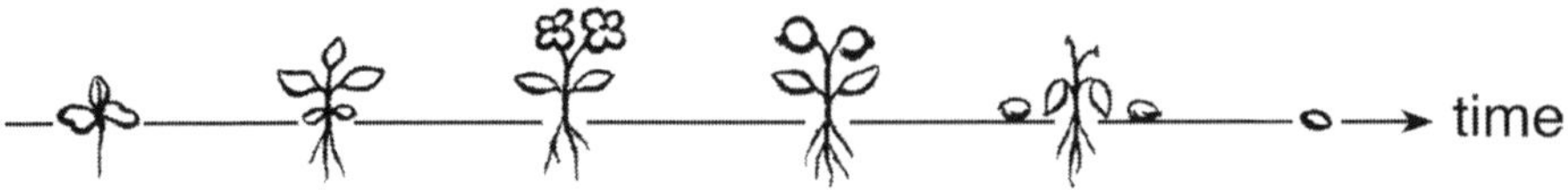

Fig. 1

before opening its flower to the sunlight, setting fruit, and finally giving the seed once more to the soil (see Fig. 1).

We should not forget that this whole process is the expression of a *being* which we name with a particular name and which *is present* at every moment of the development. Looked at as a being, we cannot speak of changes in time, for it is this being that encompasses and directs these changes according to its innate laws. We do not apply the name to a particular moment of the plant's unfolding, but to the period of its appearance as a whole. A rose is already a rose when it is just a shoot, and is also recognized as a rose when it is leafing or blossoming or forming fruit. The *being* lives at an extra-temporal and extra-spatial level; it works into our world and appears here in space and time.

We can only speak of development when the connection between being and appearance is really present in our consciousness simultaneously (see Fig. 2). Schelling, along with Goethe, was one of the first to state this clearly and unambiguously:[5]

> To the extent that every developmental process presupposes the single uniqueness of the developing subject, to that extent every [living] system has only *one* subject, *one* living element, that develops within it. In principle this means that we cannot get a firm concept of this [living thing] that is valid once and for all; for, since the system is in constant movement, progression, and augmentation, any concept can only be applicable to a single moment; as a living thing it is in fact not single but infinitely many. It can be seen from this that there is no point in a living totality [...] that one could hold or fix, but that we must simply wait for the developmental process as a whole [to finish] before a complete concept of the developing subject can be gained. For this subject is in the middle and the end and just as much at the beginning, and is not what we find at any single point of the development; it is not one thing at all, but the One and All of the totality.[6]

Another problem, one concerning methodology, was becoming increasingly important for Goethe who had made the same observation

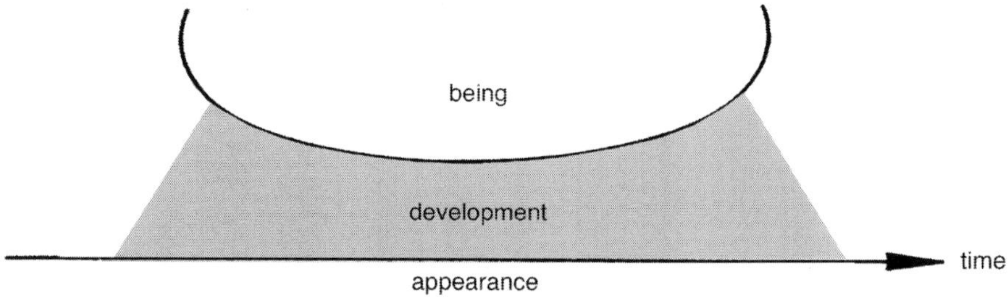

Fig. 2

for many years. He discovered that following the above stages of development requires us at the same time to develop our own faculty of mental imaging if our statements about the object are to be accurate:

> When we look at [...] all forms, particularly organic forms, we never find anything that just is, never something that is at rest and complete, but rather that everything is in a continuous state of movement. [...] What has been formed is immediately re-formed and changed, and if we wish to be able to some extent to attain a living perception of nature, we must maintain *in ourselves* as much *inner mobility and plasticity* as is in the example in which nature is at work before us.[7]

In addition, someone practising this has to learn 'to master this in their perception'. This is a laborious undertaking, and Goethe often lamented how hard it was to attain this mental participation in the productions of creative nature.

> Here we meet a difficulty in ourselves that we are not always conscious of, that between the idea and what we observe there seems to be a certain chasm which all our strength tries in vain to cross. Nevertheless it remains our eternal endeavour to overcome this hiatus, whether with reason, intellect, imagination, faith, feeling, delusion, or when all else fails, with absurdity. [...]
>
> In all research of nature, the difficulty in combining idea and observation is very troublesome; the idea is independent of space and time, whereas research is constrained within space and time; therefore simultaneity and succession are closely bound in the idea, but from the standpoint of observation they are always separate, and a process in nature which, in accordance with the idea, we need to think of as being both simultaneous and consecutive at the same time, seems to drive us into a kind of madness. The intellect cannot unite in thought what the senses give it in

> separation, and thus the quarrel between what we perceive and what we think in ideas continues unresolved.[8]

This problem was still occupying Goethe at the end of his life because he had found on innumerable occasions that his attempts to clarify it were simply not understood. On the one hand this was due to the unpractised consciousness of those who received the information, but, on the other, to the problems inherent in trying to present the question. For 'an awareness of this kind, an apprehension, mental image, concept, idea, or whatever we call it, continues to have a certain esoteric quality no matter how one approaches it. It can be spoken of in its totality, but not proved; its details can indeed be demonstrated, but then it is not full and complete.'[9]

So, if we wish to think in terms of development, there are two faculties we need to develop: the ability to follow movement consciously with our mind [to follow movement in our mental picturing], and the ability to think holistically, where at every moment we have an overview of the entire complex of interrelationships. These are exactly the abilities required by the Club of Rome but which were already necessary for the emergence of the idea of evolution. This means that the discoverers of the idea must have already practised and mastered these abilities, if only to a certain degree.

The feeling for development however, did not originally ignite in scientific observations, but in personal striving. This comes to expression perhaps most beautifully in a letter of Goethe's in which, finding himself caught in a difficult situation, he decides to set himself a goal and to develop towards it. It is a letter written by the 25-year-old Goethe to his pen-friend Gustel Stolberg at a time when his engagement to Lili Schönemann had reached crisis point:

> If you can imagine, my dear, a Goethe in fur coat, and otherwise from head to toe in passably consistent gallantry, surrounded by the insignificant splendour of the wall candles and chandeliers, amongst all kinds of people, captivated by a pair of beautiful eyes at the gaming table, driven, for a change in the diversions, from the company into the concert and from there to the ball, and with reckless interest pays court to a pretty blond; then there you have the present carnival Goethe, [...] who may not write to you, who sometimes forgets you because he finds it unbearable to be in your presence.
>
> But now there is another Goethe, in a grey beaver coat, with brown silk neckerchief and boots, who already senses spring in

> the touch of the February air, and for whom his beloved wide world will soon be open again; who, always alive, striving and working within himself, tries to express the innocent feelings of youth in short poems, or the strong spice of life in various dramas, or, as much as his skill allows, the figures of his friends and his surroundings and his beloved household things with crayon on grey paper, and asks neither to right nor left what people will think of what he does, because in his efforts he is always rising to a higher level, because he doesn't wish to jump towards ideals, but to develop his feelings, battling and playing, into new capacities—this is the one whose greatest happiness it is to live with the best individuals of his time.[10]

This letter contains one of the very first references to development, and already in the way the concept was used later. In terms of an individual—of Goethe in this case—development describes all the various forms of manifestation that will emerge, through steady striving, in the future. We can only speak of development when this striving is present, and when the goals it is aiming towards are known. In order to make progress, an evolving being needs both a relationship to the spiritual world of beings, and the availability of time and space (appearance). When the relationship to spirit is disregarded, the person's future is also lost. Goethe experienced this clearly enough in his own being, and frequently represented it in his poetic works.

Goethe found a support in this endeavour in Fichte, who, almost as soon as he was appointed at Jena University, began in his lectures to state that it is the task of every individual to develop themselves towards a self-determined goal. But this is not so simple, for:

> the care of this constant development of all a person's aptitudes and predispositions presupposes a knowledge beforehand of these in their entirety, a knowledge of all his drives and needs, that there has been an assessment of his whole being. But this complete knowledge of the whole human being is itself based on an aptitude that must be developed; for people have an urge to know, and particularly to know what is necessary for them. The development of this aptitude, however, requires all our time and energy ... But this great knowledge concerning human dispositions and needs, without a practical knowledge on how to develop and satisfy them, would not only be sad and dispiriting, it would also be empty and completely useless knowledge.[11]

Alongside an accurate knowledge of the human being with all his potential for perfection, Fichte requires here a worked-out path of practice that is intended to enable those who have this knowledge to realize the goal they are striving towards. One of the first pieces of advice that Fichte himself gives in his lectures is the following:

> Choose a definite task for yourself that you are convinced is within your power to achieve. You must do everything within the range of this task, no matter what the danger or sacrifice. You do not have energy for what is beyond this if you need it for what is within your range. Working only according to what you have planned is strong — wild enthusiasm and bragging force is always weak.[12]

This rule is typical of Fichte and reflects his whole being. However, another step is needed in this development impulse in order to enable us to carry out the task in a way that really makes sense. We have:

> to know at which cultural level the society, of which we are a member, stands at a given point of time, which level it is to ascend to from there, and what means it has for this purpose.
>
> Now, using reason based in general on all previous empirical experience, we can calculate humanity's course; we can safely state the various stages that must be passed through in order to reach a specific level of learning and culture; but it is simply impossible, using reason alone, to determine at what level it actually stands at a given time; for that we must consult observation; we must research—but with a view purified by philosophy—the world before us; we must look around us and observe our contemporaries ...[13]

Only with knowledge that presupposes a wide survey of the course of history can we ascertain what tasks for the future need to be taken up *today*, and which exercises are needed for this.

It also becomes clear from Fichte's thought that the notion of evolution works its way to the surface through the experience of the person who seeks to advance the culture he lives in, and to perfect himself. This sheds a different light on Goethe's letter to Gustel Stolberg quoted above. For to begin with Goethe is dissatisfied with the outer nature of culture in which chandeliers, a show of magnificence, and games determine life. He wants something different. He would like to grow and develop his capacities through an exchange of ideas with the best individuals of his time. All cultural development is fed by this double stream. On the one hand there are the external environmental influences with their norms of behaviour, their principles of education and training (of whatever kind), into which we grow completely naturally and almost unconsciously; but, on the other hand, there is a striving that awakens in us during this process, towards goals that are set by ourselves. When we achieve these, they in turn work back on the next generation. We could say that because Goethe worked so exceedingly hard and increased his faculties, he was able to exert an influence on his contemporaries and to change the whole of culture. We only have to think of the rapid intellectual progress that was initiated by the discovery of the idea of evolution.

The culture of every age is advanced by individuals who feel a certain tension between themselves and the culture around them, which they seek to bring into balance and harmony. This can be more or less difficult depending on one's situation in life and one's temperament, but whatever the case, there will be an effect. For this reason the elderly Goethe could write the following motto over his *Dichtung und Wahrheit* (Poetry and Truth): 'What we wish for in youth, we have in fullness in old age.' We should read this as: 'What we strive for in youth, we have in fullness in old age.'

What we see here as the basis of development for Goethe and the German idealists arises again in a similar form in Rudolf Steiner as well. He too had an intense striving towards the spirit, and he too was dissatisfied with the general scientific culture of his time. As soon as he finished secondary school, and in preparation for university, he applied himself to Fichte's *Wissenschaftslehre* (The Science of Knowledge), having 'finally come to the point of seeing in the activity of the human I the only possible point of departure for truly knowing anything. When the I is active and itself beholds this activity, then there is a spiritual element immediately present in our consciousness.'[14] Nevertheless he was not yet completely satisfied with this insight, so he went through *The Science of Knowledge* page by page and rewrote it. Through *The Science of Knowledge*, Steiner became particularly interested in Fichte's treatise *Über die Bestimmung des Gelehrten* (The Vocation of the Scholar) and *Über das Wesen des Gelehrten* (the Nature of the Scholar). He found a sort of ideal in these works that he himself wished to strive for.[15] In addition they constituted an introduction to an intensive and deepened study of Fichte's other works, which then led to Schelling and finally to Hegel. Thus prepared, he met Karl Julius Schröer at the Technical University in Vienna, who ignited his enthusiasm for Goethe. Schröer quickly discovered his student's great gifts in the realm of thought, and arranged for him to take on the editing and notes of Goethe's scientific writings for Kürschner's *Deutsche Nationalliteratur* (German national literature). This task, which Steiner took on in 1882, was the beginning of fourteen years of intensive work on Goethe, initially in Vienna and later, after the founding of the Goethe and Schiller Archive by Grand Duchess Sophie von Sachsen-Weimar-Eisenach, in Weimar. The much-praised first volume of Goethe's morphological writings appeared already in 1884 in its Kürschner *Deutsche Nationalliterature* edition, followed shortly afterwards by a detailed supplement to this in Steiner's *Grundlinien einer Erkenntnistheorie der Goetheschen Weltanschauung, mit besonderer Rücksicht auf Schiller* (Goethe's Theory of Knowledge).

Steiner had a lot to thank this task for, which came to him from outside. It is true that at the beginning his own striving had to change, but what he gained from his work on Goethe far surpassed what he had originally intended. Here was the opportunity of having to understand, and explain to a wide public, all Goethe's writings in which the connection between the sensory and the spiritual world gradually unfolded in the concept of *development* [or evolution]. In this work Steiner had to train himself to think in developmental processes to the extent that this had been done before him by Goethe and the idealists.[16] Looking back, in *The Course of My Life*,[17] Steiner describes this as follows:

> My presentation of Goethe's ideas was a struggle over a number of years to understand Goethe better and better with the help of my own thoughts. When I look back at this struggle, I must say that I have a great deal to thank it for in the development of my spiritual findings and experiences. This development happened a lot slower than it would have done if destiny had not put the Goethe task in my life's path. I would then have followed my own spiritual experiences and presented them in the way they appeared before me. I would have been pulled into the spiritual world faster; but I would have had no reason to submerse myself, struggling, into my own interior.

The idea of development, with its many layers, now became an experience for Rudolf Steiner as well. In his supplementary work on Goethe, he recognized that our own destiny is bound up with the influences of external culture through upbringing, education, and the conditions of the times; thus in his relationship to his work on Goethe he could see very vividly how karma works in human life. For:

> destiny is composed of two factors that unite into one in a human life. The one flows outward from within as an urge of the soul; the other comes towards us from the external world. The urges of my own soul tended towards perception of the spirit; the external intellectual and spiritual life of the world brought the Goethe work to me.

> I had to bring the two streams, which met in my consciousness, into harmony there. I spent the final years of the first part of my life in justifying myself alternately to myself, and to Goethe.

In this difficult balancing process, Steiner developed the required faculties of thinking, mentioned earlier, to a high degree. On the appearance side, he intensified his thinking to the point of it becoming a formative thinking that is able to follow not only sensory phenomena but finally also purely mental-spiritual constructs, concepts and ideas in their genesis. On the being side, he received insights into the spiritual worlds that bear witness to a strong overview of very broad vistas. Both these faculties were developed further in the writing of *The Philosophy of Freedom*.[18] The many years of practice in Goethe's idea of development, which was allotted to Steiner by destiny, was complemented and completed in an ideal way in Steiner's own striving towards the spirit. This becomes evident when we add a later comment woven into the course of a lecture:[19]

> I may perhaps be allowed a personal remark here, because these things can be directly linked to what is personal. I have been engaged with Goethe continuously since I was eighteen or nineteen, but I have never felt tempted to write anything genuinely historical about Goethe in the philological sense of the word or even to present it—never—for the simple reason that right from the beginning an idea was living in me, namely that the essential thing is that Goethe is alive! Not that one has in mind here the Goethe who was born in 1749 and died in 1832 as a physical man, but the important thing is that when Goethe died in 1832, not only something in his individuality continued to live, but something continues to live that is around us like the air, but spiritual, not merely in what people say, ... but spiritually surrounding us. The spiritual is around us in a way that was not yet possible for the people of ancient times. The etheric body is separated from the soul as a kind of second corpse, but, through the Christ Impulse that has remained since the Mystery of Golgotha, it is preserved in a certain sense, does not dissolve ... And when we ... believe that, as an etheric body, Goethe has risen again, and engage in a study of him, then his concepts and ideas themselves become alive in us, and we do not describe him as he was but how he is now today. Then we have brought the concept of resurrection into life. Then we believe in the resurrection. Then we can speak about believing not merely in dead thoughts but in the living and continuing working of thoughts. This is connected with a profound mystery of modern time. We can think what we may ... but as long as we

are in a physical body, our thoughts are obstructed from expressing themselves in the proper way. No matter how great Goethe was, his thoughts were greater than he himself. And the fact that they were as great as they were but not greater, is the fault of his physical body. The moment they could separate from the physical body—I mean here the thoughts that live on in a certain sense in the etheric body, not his feeling and will—and when they are taken up by someone who receives them in love and thinks them further, then they become something different, then they gain a new life. Believe that the first form in which thoughts can arise in someone is under no circumstances the last form they have; believe in a resurrection of thoughts! And believe it so firmly, that you gladly link up not merely in your blood with your ancestors, but with your spiritual soul-ancestors, and find them ... Fulfil the saying of Christ: do not only connect with the bodies in blood, but connect to souls with the spirit, then you make the idea of the resurrection effective, directly effective in life. Then you believe in the resurrection during life ... Anyone who, with their soul, follows the past in this sense, learns to experience in themselves how the past lives on. And then it is just a matter of time until the moment comes when Christ is there, when Christ is with you. Everything depends on holding fast to the Risen One and to the resurrection, and saying to ourselves: there is a spiritual world all around us, and the resurrection has had an effect! ... There is a path to the Mystery of Golgotha that can be walked inwardly ...

In short, it is *mystically* possible—in the true sense of the word—to experience the Mystery of Golgotha; but we mustn't get stuck in abstractions, but must undergo the inner experiences I just described. And if someone asks: how can I find Christ myself?—they need to be clear that they will have to meet the Risen One, and that if they have the patience and tenacity to take the path just described, at the right time they will meet Christ, and can be sure that this meeting will take place.

This 'personal' experience of Rudolf Steiner's takes our gaze beyond Goethe into completely new dimensions. Here the inner nature of Christianity began to reveal itself to him, and his subsequent activity followed in the light of this. In *The Course of My Life*, Steiner also writes that, at the end of the century, the 'true content of Christianity' as an 'inner revelation of knowledge' (*Erkenntnis-Erscheinung*) began to unfold.[20] This spiritual stream flowed into the lectures on *Christianity as Mystical Fact*, which had been requested by a circle of Berlin theosophists. With this the spiritual sources were opened, beginning with the spiritualization of thinking, and feeding finally into the abundance of spiritual-scientific presentations.

Christianity as Mystical Fact, and *Mysticism at the Dawn of the Modern Age* which was published a year before, are Steiner's first historical works. They open the broad stream of spiritual and historical themes which from the very beginning are linked, in resonance with their inner significance, to the Mystery of Golgotha.

So now we come to the threshold of our [twentieth] century, a time in which there was as yet no spiritual content and no society cultivating spiritual methods, and in which Rudolf Steiner had only to concern himself with his own development. Meanwhile, what he endeavoured to do again and again in his writing and books, was to draw people's attention to the great works of the German idealists, so that other people too, like himself, could make progress in the spiritualizing of thinking. The chief work arising entirely from these attempts, *The Philosophy of Freedom*, did not yet have the hoped-for effect, and its potential could only be recognized once enough people, by other ways, had become sensitized to 'formative thinking'. Although, after moving to Berlin, Steiner was in the thick of the general culture of his time—publishing the *Magazin für Literatur*, being active in the Giordano Bruno-Bund, teaching at the School for the Education of Workers and some other institutions, and having just written *Welt- und Lebensanschauungen im neunzehten Jahrhundert* (View of the world and of life in the nineteenth century)—he stood alone in his attempt to find individuals who were really interested in spiritual themes, and with whom he could establish a spiritual worldview. This only changed when he found people in the circle of theosophists who were really interested in him and his spiritual discoveries, who found their teacher in him, and asked him to lead the German section of the Theosophical Society. When Steiner agreed to this, a new chapter began in the spiritual history not only of this society but of our whole culture.

The Mysteries of the Light — the Evolution and Intensification of Thinking

> Anthroposophy has arisen out of the needs of *science* itself, from the course of scientific development in our age having completed its great, we could even say stupendous, victory march through the last three to four centuries. Anthroposophy arose out of this science-mindedness by attempting at the same time to carefully examine what the *Goethean worldview* can give in a fructifying way to the modern scientific spirit... I have been looking for this developmental progress for anthroposophy since the 1880s.[21]

With these words, Rudolf Steiner characterizes his impulse at the beginning of the new century when he encountered the genuine interest of the theosophists. This is noteworthy since the presumed interest in new occult information was not shared by the whole [theosophical] movement. The movement consisted of people who were engaged in art, others who were interested in religion and history, and still others who had Christianity close to their heart. Steiner was confronted with all these varied interests. But what he considered the most essential and primary necessity, was a thorough schooling in thinking as the prerequisite to deeper understanding. That he considered this element to be indispensable is already clear in the keynote lecture he gave during the founding of the German section of the Theosophical Society in the Giordano Bruno-Bund, with the theme of *Theosophy and Monism*. In order to understand what happened there, we need to look back a little.

From the moment in 1897 when Rudolf Steiner moved from Weimar to Berlin in order to take up the editing and publishing of the *Magazin für Literatur* (Magazine for literature), he participated most energetically in the cultural life of the city. He joined in with many groups, was invited to speak at certain events, led many protest demonstrations against the self-assured censorship of that time, sometimes even successfully. Thus he also joined the Giordano Bruno-Bund, founded in 1900 on the 300th anniversary of the death of this 'free thinker'. This 'association for a uniform worldview' was so that 'individuals could come together who were sympathetic towards a spiritual and monistic worldview. What was emphasized was that there are not two cosmic principles, matter and spirit, but that spirit, as a unified principle, forms all existence.'[22] What was understood as 'spirit' by the leading representatives of the association, however, could not satisfy Steiner. He found the blather 'about the spirit in general' irritating, because 'nothing was left except the word "spirit"'.[23] So, in a lecture on *Thomas Aquinas and Monism*, he decided to give his opponents some extra help by proving 'that Thomas Aquinas was a true monist. But one must not only use the term *monism* for what is understood today as materialistic monism, but must call anyone a monist who sees the cosmic principle in a *monon*, in a unity.' And Thomas Aquinas of course saw this 'in the unified divine nature ... that is behind all creation in the world.'[24]

This lecture unleashed a great deal of agitation among the members of the association. They thought Steiner was trying to open the door to Catholicism—and in Berlin, too!—attributed all sorts of other intentions to him, but did not understand him at all. 'When I gave this lecture, people really wondered if I had gone mad over night ... And these were actually the most enlightened people of the time.'[25] Once things had quietened down and the dust settled again, Steiner ventured nevertheless, and in the Giordano Bruno-Bund, to give his 'founding anthroposophical lecture' which became the starting point of all his anthroposophical activity.

The setting for this most important milestone in the development of anthroposophy was not the founding meeting of the German Theosophical Society, in which Rudolf Steiner was confirmed in the office of general secretary, but in a public lecture and on the scientific ground of the Giordano Bruno Association. Even the title, *Monism and Theosophy*, already promised to be highly controversial, and so the talk was well attended. How much more astounding it must have been for the listening audience when the speaker set out the reasons why a viable worldview can only be established on the basis of modern science.[26] What was meant here was certainly a natural science that also understood itself in connection with Goethe and German idealism, a science that took *evolution* seriously, spiritually speaking, and did not simply confuse it with change. Steiner had already explained this in his little booklet on *Haeckel und seine Gegner* (Haeckel and his opponents), in which he came to Haeckel's aid, who had used the term 'monism' rather loosely. After describing the nature of this modern science, Steiner turns to a thinker who, despite his outstanding significance, was already forgotten by that time: Immanuel Hermann Fichte (1796-1879).

In 1833, this great son of a great father, under the harmless title of *Erkennen als Selbsterkenntnis* (knowledge as self-knowledge), had for the first time observed and described 'the scientific history of the development of consciousness *to* and *in* thinking'. He traces the various stages of consciousness, from the infant and, via a perceiving and mental-picturing consciousness, to the thinking I. This last stage can also be surpassed through practice when the I learns to observe itself as a thinking being and realizes that '*even thinking is thought by itself*'. This step is one of the boldest and most important in the entire development of consciousness and is worthy of the greatest wonder 'because it suddenly opens up a new world, because in it the spirit [or mind] has first emancipated itself to have thoughts that are speculative—(that is,) thoughts it creates out of itself'.[27] When this act, which can only take place in freedom, is really carried out and observed in the execution, thinking lifts itself to 'intellectual perception' (*intellektualen Anschauung*) or, as Fichte called it, to 'knowing through speculative perception' (*spekulativ anschauenden Erkennen*), and this lives in the beholding of the eternal divine spirit. This is the point where philosophy, thought by means of normal thinking, makes a transition into *theosophy*, into 'knowledge of the divine Spirit as mirrored in its works'. The way I H Fichte characterizes theosophy—that is, as knowledge arising through a further development of thinking that never contrasts itself against a dead object, but is itself 'essentially the *immanent genesis* and presenting *unfolding* of what is to be known'—is also how Rudolf Steiner would like the theosophy of a Theosophical Society to be understood. He sees the task of such a society to be the cultivation of an intensification of thinking, the foundations for which were laid in Goethe's time and then systematized by I H Fichte. The great value that Steiner placed on this can be seen from the end of this noteworthy lecture of 8 October 1902, in which he emphasizes once more the unity between a science broadened in this way, and the spirit, and strongly rejects all abnormal and mystical inclinations of the soul-life. Looking back on this a few days later, he again characterizes his intention in a private letter to a theosophist:

> Everything will now depend on being able to work in a way that is not compromised by the connection to the theosophical movement. I knew what I was risking on that evening ... I am certainly under no illusions, but I think that, for the most part, those who were there went away with an awareness that they were now standing before something they shouldn't pass by. ... The people in the Giordano Bruno Association know me as someone who knows about science ... I came to the audience with *genuine German theosophy*. The middle section of my lecture was an interpretation of a sentence written by I H Fichte in 1833.[28]

This lecture was intended as a keynote lecture for future aims, and Mrs Besant, the then leader of the Theosophical Society, was informed of its content so that there could be no doubt as to the direction in which Steiner wanted to go. He was given freedom to teach what he wanted, and so the first phase of the anthroposophical society's development was begun, still entirely within the Theosophical Society. However, it was evident right from the start that western theosophy was dealing with a spiritual life that was somewhat different from what was otherwise cultivated in the broader society. For, in the traditional Theosophical Society there was what one could call a more eastern theosophy, but Rudolf Steiner very consciously opposed this. In hindsight twenty years later, it was seen like this:

> During the first phase...the Anthroposophical Society led a kind of embryonic life within the Theosophical Society. ... It had its own particular task during this first phase: it had the task of countering what was to be found in the Theosophical Society—which was the absorption of primordial oriental wisdom—with the spirituality of occidental civilization with the Mystery of Golgotha at its centre.[29]

How little this had been understood in 1902 can be seen from a humorous remark made by Steiner when speaking about the founding meeting of the Theosophical Society. He had to interrupt the meeting because of a lecture he had to give as part of a related cycle on the theme of '*Von Zarathustra bis Nietzsche—Entwicklungsgeschichte der Menschheit an Hand der Weltanschauungen von den ältesten orientalischen Zeiten bis zur Gegenwart, oder Anthroposophie*' (From Zarathustra to Nietzsche—history of human development with reference to the worldviews of the most ancient oriental times up to the present, or anthroposophy). Afterwards, 'one of the theosophists who later became a good anthroposophist came up to me and said, "Yes, but what you said doesn't concur with what Mrs Besant says or what Blavatsky says." And I said, "Then that must indeed be the case." This was someone well acquainted with all the dogmas of theosophy, who noticed correctly: that doesn't concur. Already at that time one could say: No, that doesn't concur; it is something different.'[30]

However, this 'something different' would not have developed without the stimulus from the Orient. By setting up western spirituality, Rudolf Steiner answers the question from the East. Without this, the whole process might not have got going. But now, with the German section of the Theosophical Society established, and Steiner as its general secretary, the flood gates of spiritual knowledge were opened, which provided the foundation for the anthroposophical movement.

First of all Steiner set up the magazine *Luzifer*, in which he developed the central themes of this agenda. Right at the beginning his famous essays appeared there on '*Reinkarnation und Karma, vom Standpunkt der modernen Naturwissenschaft notwendige Vorstellungen*' (Reincarnation and karma from the standpoint of aspects needed by modern science), which were revised and extended in his book *Theosophy* in 1904. It is, in a sense, Rudolf Steiner's special concern in his research to really clarify the concept of destiny and to introduce this into occidental culture. Nowhere does he resort to eastern sources for this, but endeavours to reveal this difficult subject—which Goethe had striven for in vain his whole life—through his own observation of the facts and using scientific methods, an undertaking that accompanied him throughout his life. Even his final lectures and *Letters to Members* were still opening up new aspects of this inexhaustible but also very difficult theme.

In other articles and innumerable lectures it is as though the entire edifice of anthroposophy is erected with one great stroke, and elucidated from the most varied sides. The path of self-schooling is systematically described, research is done into the pre- and post-existent life of the human being and his reincarnation, and the evolution of the earth and the cosmos is investigated, and so on; and all this is done with the background of 'the historical development within human existence on earth that has its centre in the Mystery of Golgotha and in the Christ Impulse'.[31] Steiner also managed in this construction phase to make a transition from the more external research which relied chiefly on the available literature—similar to the methods used in his book *Christianity as Mystical Fact*—to a more internal research method that included reading the akashic chronicle. Rudolf Steiner became more and more confident in taking what he saw and translating it into the form of thoughts, so that every lecture contained new findings. Thus, for example, the ancient mysteries were gradually deciphered even into the content of their teaching and their path of training, a modus operandi that discovered occult facts by, as it were, observing what happened during the ancient initiations. For looking in the 'earth's memory', and researching the content of the past mysteries, reveals those truths there which still interest us deeply today. Alongside the many public and internal lectures which incorporated this wealth of new findings, Marie von Sivers now organizes for them to be printed. This initially involved the printing and distribution of single lectures, but then also of lecture cycles recorded by a stenographer and printed in provisional form. This is followed by collections in book form of Steiner's articles for *Luzifer* and *Luzifer-Gnosis* (e.g. *Knowledge of the Higher Worlds—How is it Achieved?* 1909). This steady unfolding of spiritual science is crowned by *Occult Science—An Outline* in 1910. Those who were involved in these early stages of anthroposophy were amazed not only at the wealth of the spiritual stream that had the potential to lay the foundations for a spiritual culture of the future, but also became aware, with the continuing revelations, that a spiritual life of this nature was one that opened up possibilities for their own participation. In the long run, one could not just let these interesting lectures flow over one without working on them, without at least noticing for oneself the consequences that a spiritual life of this nature actually required. The initially delicate impulse towards transforming one's own soul-life began to exert an influence.

In order to meet this impulse, Rudolf Steiner founded the so-called 'Esoteric School' in 1904. Something of this kind had already been envisioned in the Theosophical Society, and intended for those members who wished to cultivate a meditative spiritual life. Here, at regular intervals, Steiner gave instruction for a meditative life[32]—sometimes even to individuals who had requested it—and elucidated more subtle aspects of history from an esoteric perspective. However, the more comprehensively the schooling path and its conditions became publicly available, the more reticent Steiner became in giving further instruction in the Esoteric School until, at the beginning of the First World War, he closed it altogether.

When we survey the first phase of the Anthroposophical Society's development, we can understand why this was called the 'scientific phase' by Rudolf Steiner. He tried at this time to present all the facts that were discussed and described, in such a way that they could be understood by a healthy thinking engaged in meditative development. Initially he connected this exclusively with the mental and psychological faculties that had developed in the European context over the centuries, and which were stimulated to further development by the German idealists. Grasping the world conceptually, however, goes back originally to Greek culture and its mysteries. It is here that the specifically European intellectual life was ignited, with its logical thought forms and its abstract concepts. Steiner refers to this on many occasions:

> The intellectual life of our culture, in the form it presents itself to someone who really accepts things externally ... is absorbed by people through the influence working on them through the continuation of ancient Greek and Roman culture ... that flowed into what later became our grammar schools, what became our universities. For all our so-called humanist education right down to our primary schools is completely dependent on what flowed into it as a stream of Greek elements. For, our intellectual life, our European intellectual life, has Greek origins that then passed through Latin influences.[33]

It certainly began to change then [through the Roman influence]—which continued into the Middle Ages—but it came originally from Greek culture. It was in Greece that the thought forms were developed that we apply even today, and there that the abstract concepts were first thought that we still make use of as a matter of course. But the deeper origin of Greek thought leads us further into the past and into the ancient Orient. However, 'over there in the Orient, this spiritual culture was significantly more spiritual than it was in Greece, and in the Orient it was an outflow of what we can call the *mysteries of the spirit*, or I could also say the *mysteries of the Light*'.[34]

The great Greek philosophers, who were still closely associated with the mystery centres, made essential strides on the path from a spiritual life founded on the ancient mystery schools to one based on thinking. Among them was Heraclitus of Ephesus, and Plato who as an Athenian was initiated into the mysteries of Eleusis; then there was the northern Greek, Aristotle, who was connected to the Macedonian mystery centre of Samothrace, and a few others. European intellectual life was particularly influenced by the logical writings of Aristotle, not only during the Middle Ages but beyond these right into our own time. His categories, such as *space, time, position, doing, being affected*, etc., are comprehensive concepts which, in the final analysis, are behind all intellectual investigation. Rudolf Steiner described in a later lecture[35] what influences from the mysteries in Samothrace had been necessary for Aristotle to 'remember' his former initiation in the mysteries of Ephesus, and establish from this experience 'the cosmic script ... with thoughts' whose letters are the ten categories. With these one could have learnt to read the cosmos, if one had given it attention. Indeed, Steiner goes even further when he says:

> And, fundamentally, what has produced anthroposophy, and can always produce it, is experienced in these concepts [Aristotle's categories] in the same way that what is read in *Faust* is experienced through the letters. For, all the mysteries of the physical and spiritual world are contained in these simple concepts of the cosmic alphabet.[36]

Various works by Aristotle, for example his *Psychology* and the *Nicomachean Ethics*, also established a mental-spiritual foundation for an understanding of the Christ being. According to Aristotle, the highest goal of the human being is the *divine human* who, as the mediator between the divine and the human worlds, participates in both. What the natural human being needed to do in order to develop this was all researched by Aristotle in painstaking detail. And Rudolf Steiner recommends the study of these investigations as part of our efforts to gain an understanding of the Christ Being:

> Perhaps the easiest way we can approach and enter into the Mystery of Golgotha, into an understanding of the Mystery of Golgotha, is to form a picture for ourselves of how Aristotle, who stood at the apex of Greek thought, formed his picture of the soul. For Aristotle was also the leading philosopher of the Middle Ages, and our present thinking is still fed by medieval concepts.[37]

What is astonishing here is the fact that one of the leading medieval philosophers, Thomas Aquinas, had no qualms about discussing the heathen Aristotle in his discourses, understood him better than the already fairly corrupted texts of that time admit, and defended him as though he were a Christian writer. In Aquinas' later work, *On the Unity of the Intellect*,[38] Aristotle is quoted, for example, 114 times in the first chapter, whereas Plato is mentioned in the same chapter only twice. 'There is something so significant in these things, that we really must try to look at them with an open mind.'[39] As an aside here we could mention that Rudolf Steiner did exactly the same thing in his turbulent lecture in the Giordano Bruno Association.

What originated in Greek thought was then lifted to a new level by German idealism—on the one hand, by the discovery of the concept of development or evolution, a concept as yet unknown to Aristotle and to Greek thought in general, but which had consequences in all of science, and on the other hand, because thinking itself now entered the arena of observable 'objects' capable of evolution. Because of this, the purely spiritual world was now open to spiritual investigation. When I H Fichte himself had the impression that Greek philosophy was reborn in modern philosophy at a higher and more profound level,[40] he is expressing an accurate sense for the truth of the matter. Strangely enough, all the outstanding representatives of German idealism in this area had a strong relationship to ancient Greece. They do not only work on taking Greek thought further, but feel connected with it and the mysteries behind it, as though they had been there themselves. Hegel 'remembers' Eleusis; Schelling, the mysteries of Samothrace; I.H. Fichte, Plato and Aristotle; Goethe, Ephesus, and so on.

To begin with, Rudolf Steiner also consciously linked anthroposophy to this Greek mystery stream that continued to have an effect, and then developed it further from there. Someone joining the Theosophical Society in the early years could feel themselves as though participating in the former 'Lesser Mysteries' of Greece; they were taught, as happened there, about the world, and if they fulfilled the necessary purifications in their soul-life, they could expect in the future, as in the 'Greater Mysteries', to develop their own perception.

When Carl Julius Schröer wrote his Foreword to Rudolf Steiner's first volume of commentary on the works of Goethe,[41] he emphasized that the new life of thought had risen to the height it had because 'the mind' had pierced through to 'an immediate perception of antiquity' and 'carried this further with rejuvenated senses'. What Goethe achieved, Schröer writes, was 'a life of thought that continued the spirit of ancient Hellas, but which, in contrast to the ageing times, arose as something new, something that comprehended the world with original sensibility'. And thus he greets with joy the editorial undertaking of Rudolf Steiner to write a commentary on Goethe's scientific work and to 'estimate it in relation to Goethe's whole being'. For Goethe did not only have a rejuvenating effect on the nation through his poetry; he was also destined to have an influence on the currents of science. His scientific writings reveal the deep background of his intellectual and spiritual life, and his poetry draws our interest towards his research. He has already had an enormous influence on our education for a whole century, but our understanding of him increases every day, and so his influence must become even greater in the future, and particularly his scientific writings.

This continuation and elevation of ancient thought through the works of the German idealists and, following on from them, through Rudolf Steiner, is not just a matter of content in thought life; the spiritual originators of it are still connected with it. When Steiner was working on his interpretation of Goethe's thought, he had Goethe 'constantly at his side in spirit like an admonisher,' who endeavoured unceasingly to develop him further and educate him.[42] The same happened in connection with Schelling who, through his writings on the Samothracian mysteries, came 'exceptionally close' to Steiner.[43] It is not only Steiner's clairvoyant abilities that shine out behind descriptions like these; they conceal a fact that can be of significance for everyone, and which does not only follow from Steiner's 'personal remark' quoted above,[44] but from all the descriptions of the human being's life after death. For, 'the human soul continues to develop even once it has passed through the portal of death. This human soul ... grows in its forces of understanding even after death; it learns to understand more and more.' This fundamental law is discussed by Steiner here in order to show how Christianity took root and spread in humanity in early Christian times. He continues:

> Now the strange thing is that Christ's contemporaries, who through their love of Christ had prepared themselves for a life in Christ after

> death, only understood the Mystery of Golgotha fully, out of their own human forces, in the third century after the Mystery of Golgotha. In other words, the individuals who lived at the same time as Christ as his disciples and apostles, died and lived on in the spiritual world. And while they were living in the spiritual world, their forces grew just as they grow here. When we die we are not so advanced with our understanding as we are two hundred years after our death. Christ's contemporaries had only developed sufficiently in the second or towards the third century, so that, in the spiritual world in which the human being lives between death and a new birth, they came by themselves to an understanding of what they had experienced on the earth two to three centuries earlier. And then, from the spiritual world, they inspired people who were down here on the earth.[45]

The same also applies to everyone today. Someone who gives a lot of thought to the spiritual world continues to work on this after death and is then able to inspire individuals working with the same questions. All intellectual and spiritual life lives through the advances in understanding made by those who have died, although the individuals affected by this, not being clairvoyant, are mainly unaware of its origin. This source of inspiration can be strengthened when people work in community on spiritual questions; such an increase in intensity attracts many of the deceased who once occupied themselves with similar questions. A society that feels duty bound to seek the truth never consists only of its earthly members; it also consists of the deceased who were formerly connected with it. This should never be forgotten when it comes to discussions about statutes!

Anthroposophy and the Anthroposophical Society were very consciously linked by Steiner to the mystery stream of Greece whose influence lives on today, and were developed further from there. Many of the deceased are involved here. If we become aware of this, the task Rudolf Steiner set himself from 1902 onwards becomes somewhat clearer when he says he wants to counterbalance 'the absorption of primordial oriental wisdom ... with the spirituality of occidental civilization with the Mystery of Golgotha at its centre'. Under 'primordial oriental wisdom' we can also understand the wisdom of the Mysteries of the Light together with its further development in Greek thought; we can see how this is taken up again in the great surge of the idealists during Goethe's time, and observe how they develop it further both in life and in the life after death, and are ready to inspire those who come after them when those individuals themselves begin to cultivate a higher life of thought. This phase can be described as a quiet striving for wisdom. Externally, the society appeared only as an organizer of lectures in which Steiner endeavoured to extend the circle of interested people. Beyond this, a few books served as the groundwork for initial study that could be deepened through membership of the Esoteric School. However, because it was a living spiritual life that was cultivated here, tendencies soon emerged that were looking for a more will-oriented type of activity, and Rudolf Steiner also met this need: in the very middle of the first phase of the Anthroposophical Society's development the seeds were laid for the second phase. As a whole, however, the work of the society still carried on as though behind the scenes; it was of course in public view in the form of lectures, but what it was talking about concerned a change in thinking and inner transformation of the individual, and did not yet seem to touch cultural norms in general. This only changed during the second phase of its development, and then so significantly that it was plain for anyone to see.

The Mysteries of Space — Experiencing the Spiritual through Art

Up to now we have seen that, in the building up of the Anthroposophical Society, Rudolf Steiner saw his task to be to counterbalance 'what was to be found in the Theosophical Society ... with the spirituality of occidental civilization with the Mystery of Golgotha at its centre'.[46] For this he could link up with the ideas that had their seed in German idealism and were already partly developed there as well. Within their circle of friends, Goethe, Fichte, Schelling, and Hegel were the intellectual giants that Steiner lovingly studied, and was glad to connect to. Naturally, much of what Steiner gave came from his own spiritual research, but he always bore in mind the historical context, and conveyed his content right from the beginning in a way that could be understood by any thinking person. So work went on quietly towards a more developed spiritual life, and anyone who was interested could attend the public lectures or also, if they so wished, the internal group lectures within the Theosophical Society. All Steiner had to do was convey 'what could be said as a result of this honestly attained foundation of knowledge'.[47]

This changed in the second phase of the Anthroposophical Society's development. Now Steiner wanted to encourage the members to absorb anthroposophy as manifested in artistic works as well. This impulse was introduced at the Munich congress in 1907, and from then onwards, through the Mystery Dramas, the Soul Calendar, the Goetheanum building and eurythmy, the new art of movement, it did indeed come to life in many of the members, so that they were involved in this development of the arts themselves. Naturally the flow of lectures also continued, but with changed aims. Laying the foundations of anthroposophy was no longer in the foreground, but rather it was 'to survey everything that made up the outer science and practical civilization of the present. It had to be shown how anthroposophy can be brought into harmony with modern science, with the modern arts—naturally in a deeper sense—and with practical life.'[48]

The official beginning of this impulse is usually regarded as the so-called 'Munich Congress'. In 1907 the annual congress of the Theosophical Society took place in Germany, and Rudolf Steiner used the occasion to give external shape to artistic thoughts he had had living in

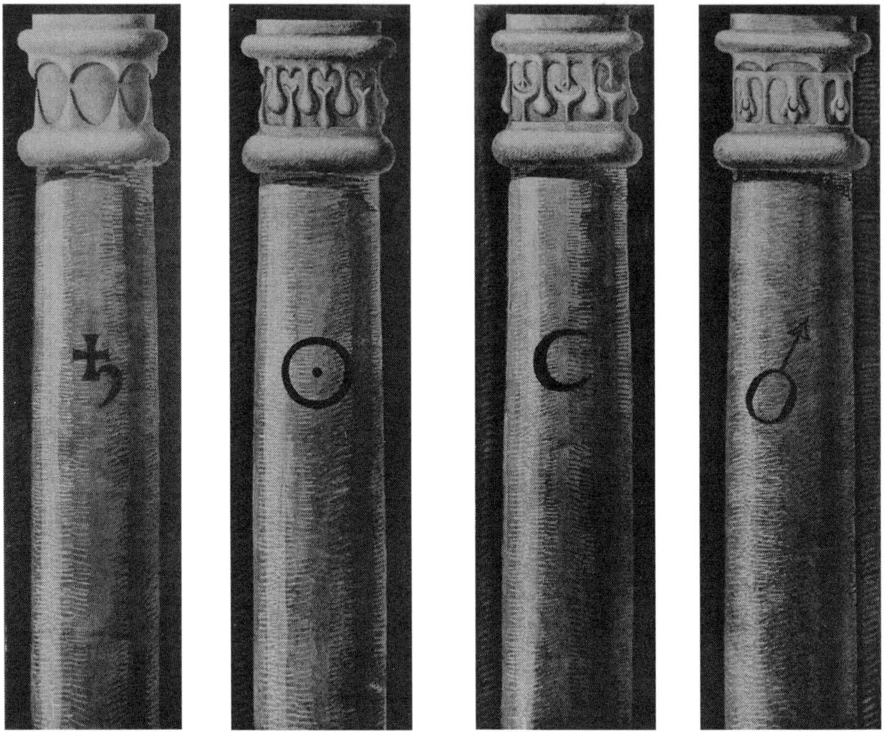

him for a long time. Already in 1905 he wrote to Marie von Sivers: 'Our ideal should be to create forms as the expression of the inner life. For in a time that is unable to behold forms and in beholding to create them, the spirit must of necessity evaporate into an abstraction with no true being, and reality in the light of this merely abstract spirit must see itself as a spiritless aggregation of matter. Once people are really able to understand forms, ... then there will soon no longer be any material for them that is devoid of spirit.'[49]

In Munich this ideal was put into practice in multiple ways. The congress participants who had travelled to Munich to listen to lectures in the usual way, found themselves unexpectedly in a hall completely hung with red drapery. The walls were decorated with seven large painted seals whose motifs were taken, on the one hand, from the Christian tradition of the Revelation of John and, on the other hand, from 'the esoteric spiritual stream which has been the leading one in the Occident since the fourteenth century'.[50] (See Fig. 4.) 'A column had been placed between each of the seals. It had not yet been possible to sculpt these seven columns so, by way of substitute, pictures had been painted on them. But they are really intended to be architectural forms and correspond to the "seven columns"

Fig. 3

of the "true Rosicrucian temple".'[51] The capitals of the seven columns show seven stages of a complete developmental process whose metamorphoses, however, are not easy to understand (see Fig. 3). Every line and every curve of these forms was shaped so that 'one awoke sleeping forces in one's soul when one was absorbed by the thing; and these forces lead to thoughts of the great cosmic mysteries that lie behind cosmic evolution and the evolution of humanity that is bound up with it'.[52]

There was more to surprise the participants at the front of the stage where the busts of Fichte, Schelling and Hegel had been placed alongside two round pillars painted red and blue-red. These two pillars are actually part of the symbolism of Solomon's Temple, which was also indicated by the two letters J and B (Jachin and Boaz), that were painted on them. But in order to elucidate their significance for the Rosicrucians, Steiner reached back to the so-called Golden Legend. He led from this to the words of the verses he had had written on the two pillars. On the one pillar were the words [literal translation]:

In pure thought you find
The Self that can maintain itself.

Fig. 4 Grail seal = 7th Seal.

If you transform thought into image
You experience creative wisdom.

And on the other pillar was written:

If you condense feeling into light,
You reveal formative power.

If you reify will into being,
You create in cosmic existence.

Although here and in the lectures during the congress Steiner was making a connection to the most ancient spiritual knowledge, it was clear from the context that only a modern life of thought that had absorbed the achievements of Fichte, Schelling, and Hegel, was in a position to unite wisdom and life. For the words of the one verse relate to the attainment of knowledge, and those of the other, to life.

Alongside the architectural, painted, and sculptural design of the room, the Munich Congress diverged from the usual congress format hitherto, with other artistic events. The lectures were accompanied by a wealth of recitation and musical contributions; and the climax of the whole event was a reconstruction of *The Sacred Dramas of Eleusis* by Edouard Schuré, designed and adapted by Steiner. In this complete permeation by the artistic element, from the design of the events to the tickets, the Munich Congress was a decisive moment in the development of the anthroposophical work. It was planned in the hope of becoming something that in the future could be continued and improved upon, and thus the invitation says: 'It is particularly important at the present time that as many people as possible participate in the congress. We are perhaps standing before important decisions in theosophical matters, and the Congress, if the opportunity is not missed, will be able to contribute a good deal towards bringing about a favourable turn of events for spiritual matters. It is therefore hoped that no member of the Society, who is at all able to attend, will be missing from this important event.'[53]

The cryptic formulation of the last sentences is to be seen as having a double meaning. For, indeed, from the Munich Congress onwards, not only did the artistic impulse gradually establish itself in the society, but vehement opposition was also aroused against a deepening of spiritual science in this form. From then onwards the path of the more eastern-oriented Theosophical Society began to separate from the path of the future Anthroposophical Society. Looking back at the event 28 years later, Marie Steiner saw this clearly when the effects of the congress were evident to her:

> The reality of these active forces was so strong that they could become the impulses which, on the one hand, like a gladdening gift from the spirit, made possible the festive production of the Mystery plays and, on the other hand, led to the bold decision to create a worthy framework for them and for what Rudolf Steiner had to say, to give them a building of their own. In the design of the Congress of 1907 ... there already lay the seed of what has now become the annual production of the plays and the Dornach building, which was initially intended for Munich. But this was also the beginning of the separation from the Theosophical Society ... The theosophists refused to accept the introduction of occidental and Christian esotericism in both its ancient and new forms.[54]

Just how different the Munich Congress was in content in comparison with other similar events, is most evident in Steiner's efforts to 'bring everything to expression in a single unified theosophical idea'. The lectures and the drama, the pictures on the seven columns and the reference to the German idealists, were all intended to be drawn from the same spiritual source. Of course, this was not always achieved. This is why Steiner sought—in asides, in additional remarks in his lectures, and in a final lecture specially included for the purpose—to elucidate the stated intentions and to show how they fitted within a greater context.

The first opportunity for this came in his first lecture to the Congress, on 'Rosicrucian Initiation', which he began with a quote from Hegel. This spoke again and again of the gradual evolution of humanity in the course of history towards a consciousness of freedom. What this means, however, only becomes clear when we look at the differentiation in humanity's progress. For 'it is only possible to recognize one's own epoch if one knows at which point in human evolution one is standing'. Thus Rudolf Steiner begins with a retrospect of Egyptian wisdom, and compares 'what the Egyptian priest, the servant of Hermes, saw when he looked up to the starry heavens', with the materialistic science of today and its findings. At that time, he says, people regarded the world physiognomically, they looked through matter to the soul element that was revealing itself within it. 'This seeing through matter to the soul-spiritual content of the soul was what the servant of Hermes meant when he said: everything below is like what is above—there is nothing material that is not the expression of a soul-spiritual element!'[55]

Later on in the lecture the Christian and gnostic path is described, as found in St John's Gospel, and its further development in Rosicrucian initiation. The first stage of this is a living in pure thought in the way it lit up, for example, in Hegel. Steiner was able to connect with this and write his *Philosophy of Freedom*. For 'this pure thinking does not arise from objects, but flows from thought to thought. For people who want to accustom themselves to a thinking completely free of sensory content, I attempted to write a book like my *Philosophy of Freedom*. It is not a personal work. It arose like an organism; it is a thought-organism and instructive guidance for what is called "study" in the Rosicrucian sense.'[56]

In his *Philosophy of Freedom*, Steiner did not only express what he held to be correct, but did this in a form which, when seen spiritually, corresponds to the same laws that a living organism is subject to! And an organism is subject, for example, to the law of evolution. We already get an inkling that the forms on the seven capitals of the columns 'decorating' the Congress hall, being pillars of a 'Rosicrucian temple', followed the same law as well.

In the afternoon of the same day there followed a performance of the *Sacred Drama of Eleusis*, a mystery play by Edouard Schuré which

Marie von Sivers had translated in prose, but which Steiner rendered into rhythms. He allowed himself a lot of freedom in this. The figure of Hermes, who opens and closes the prologue of the play, enters with the words [literal translation]:

Bethink the seer's word of ancient time:
Arising in the flow of time
Is dying for the eternities.
Man fell from the heights of the gods
Into earthly error and earthly illusion;
But memory of his origin
Can give him the essence of all truth,
Can shape him into a Son of God
In a body of earth, in existence in time.

Anyone who had attended Steiner's lecture that morning, heard these Hermetic words now in the same context in which a servant of Hermes in Egypt experienced them when he was initiated. It was intended as a mystery play, a drama, that wanted to call up images in the audience of earlier times.

Steiner's second lecture, on 'Planetary and Human Evolution', deepened the relationship of the human being with his past, so that, in addition to his existence in an earthly body, there could also dawn a knowledge of his existence in time.

Finally, on the third day, Rudolf Steiner spoke about the evolution of humanity, choosing the décor and design of the Congress hall as the imaginative underground of his presentations, and now lifted everything that had been perceived more unconsciously over the last few days, into consciousness. After discussing the colour, the deeper meaning of the two pillars, and the seven seals, he pointed to the seven 'planetary columns', the motifs of whose capitals have specific meaning down to the smallest detail. 'If you have a sculptural sense for how what is above inclines towards what is below, feelings will arise in you that give information about the streams in the respective conditions of these heavenly bodies.' Moving from Saturn existence and via Old Sun to Old Moon, the 'idea of humanity's evolution' could be experienced in the forms of the capitals, because they are an *expression of inner spiritual life*. 'What is living in the soul should shine back to us from outside, then we have done our work in accordance with cosmic development.'[57]

So, what Rudolf Steiner had seen fairly recently as his task, namely 'to create forms as the expression of inner life',[58] he attempted to realize now for the first time at the Munich Congress. He himself admitted that the seed of this wish had not yet succeeded, which is why 'we should not speak so much about what we have achieved but rather about what we intended. For the organizers are only too aware of how what has been achieved falls short of the goals that one sets oneself for an event such as this.' But still, the seed had been sown; one just had to wait to see if it would sprout.

The Malsch Building Model and the Society house in Stuttgart

For the time being the impulse lay dormant. Nevertheless, Schuré's mystery dramas had made such an impression that from then onwards a similar sort of play was produced annually, and Munich remained the centre of this artistic work. Then in 1910 Steiner himself began to write mystery dramas, an impulse that developed more and more magnificently until the beginning of the First World War. Many members who were involved with the plays, found that being personally engaged in this way gave them a growing opportunity to deepen their anthroposophy, and ensured the continued production of the 'festive plays'.[59]

But the idea of building a temple was also still alive. E.A. Karl Stockmeyer was the first to consult Steiner regarding the architecture of the columns, and received indications that were even made into a small building model in Malsch in 1908/09. This created an elliptical room whose longitudinal axis enclosed seven columns along its sides that had the sequence of capitals seen in Munich (Fig. 5). They bore a cupola in the form of a triaxial ellipsoid, and created a gallery separated from the main space. Steiner had pictured this as an underground rock temple, like the one Goethe imagined in his *Fairy Tale*, a temple that neither showed itself externally nor could be seen from outside. The temple was to be lit by a window in the cupola set up in such a way that on the solstices the light of the rising sun would fall on the Saturn column. The measure of significance that Rudolf Steiner attributed to taking up this impulse and to the Malsch model, is nowhere clearer than in the ceremonial laying of the foundation stone that he conducted for this modest building.

Steiner expected a serviceable building that would be adequate for the small 'lodge' at Malsch, and carefully marked the [foundation stone] document with 'two dragons biting their own tails. A white, winged dragon above, and below a desiccated, dark one. On the right, written below each other, the words "Everything above as below",

Fig. 5. Building model at Malsch.

again the Hermetic words.'[60] After all those present had signed the document, it was put in a jar and laid in the ground beneath the foundation stone. This was followed by a short address on the significance, in earlier times and today, of laying foundation stones, and finished with a petition for blessing.

After Malsch, the building impulse continued in Stuttgart. Here, a generous donation of a sizeable sum (ca. 46,500 Marks), made it possible to think of building the society's own house. A small building association was formed on 20 May 1910 who pursued the plan energetically. Already on 1 October 1910, a joint decision was made in a general meeting of the three Stuttgart branches to have their own home. Steiner had been informed of this plan beforehand and had agreed to come to Stuttgart for the laying of the foundation stone. This then took place on 3 January 1911 following a cycle of lectures on *Occult History.*[61] Steiner felt so warmly received by the audience during these lectures, that he ventured for the first time to talk about what was really important to him. This had not been possible anywhere until now. So he spoke about individual connections of destiny over a number of incarnations (Gilgamesh and Eabani, Alexander the Great and Aristotle, and so on) from the aspect of the further world-historic tasks of each of them. Due to the friendly atmosphere in Stuttgart, Rudolf Steiner and Marie von Sivers decided to organize a flat of their own in the building of the branch house in Landhausstrasse [70]. Thus the building association's minute book records on 8 January 1911, that a two-room flat for Frl. v. Sivers and Dr Steiner should be included in the plans. Through this decision, Rudolf Steiner had found another centre for his work, alongside Berlin and later also Dornach.

On 15 October 1911 a ceremony was held to dedicate the house. The large lecture hall, which had its own subtle inner design and was painted blue, was filled to capacity with around 500 guests. With great expectations, Adolf Arenson invited Rudolf Steiner 'to dedicate the place of our future work'. This then happened in a most unusual way. To begin with, Steiner called to mind the 'devoted theosophical work' that had been done here, the peaceful collaboration between the different branches and the generosity of the donors. Then he emphasized the particularly active work of the smaller building association: 'The work that we stand before today is in the fullest sense a magnificent justification of the trust we placed in the faithful work of the small building association that has been active here. With trust and understanding we express our thanks for

Fig. 6. Invitation to the house opening in Stuttgart.

the exemplary work of the building association.' The building association consisted of only a few members, amongst whom the greatest workload was borne for many years by José del Monte, Carl Unger, Emil Molt, and W Schrack. Steiner goes on to say how it is significant for him that this first building of the society had come about in an area which was closely connected in the time of German idealism with a true striving for the spirit. It was here in 1791 that Hölderlin 'wrote these three words in the family album of a friend: One in All ...[62] Often put the other way round, these words were written in this region out of a deep sensibility. They were written in the album of a man whose philosophical mind filled all Germany and, fundamentally, the whole educated world.'[63]

The fact that Rudolf Steiner focuses on this remarkable *hen kai pan* [Greek: 'one and all'], does not only tie in with his emphasis on the link between anthroposophy and the stream of western spirituality which had its origins precisely in this region, and from which 'the great philosophers were sent out'; more significant for him is that the *hen kai pan* appears as an inscription to the primordial symbol of a snake biting its own tail (Fig. 8). It had already been written into the foundation stone in Malsch, and here in Stuttgart only those who knew about it were reminded of it.
This introduction is followed by the actual dedication of the 'temple building'. Steiner had selected a few characteristic extracts from the

Fig. 7 Lecture hall of the Stuttgart branch house.

Old Testament for this, which describe the dedication of the Temple of Solomon:

> O Spirit of the Universe, You who proclaim Yourself to our true self-awareness (*Selbsterkenntnis*), You have graciously received the word which You gave us, in that You saw our work as carried out by Your servants over years; and it becomes manifest today at this hour ... Look down to us, Spirit of the Universe, Permeater of every I, and may Your eye be open over this building, where You have decided to dwell ...[64]

Fig. 8

This 'prayer' in Solomonic words to the spirit of the universe sounded very strange in the context of what was still the theosophical movement at that time, particularly considering that the building being dedicated here was no temple but consisted of only a large lecture hall and a few rooms. At any rate, that is how everyone who came to the dedication saw it at the time. In reality, however, there was a beautifully designed second hall below the ground floor, which had been built underground similar to the Malsch model, and which only the building association knew about. For everything necessary for its construction—the columns, the ceiling paintings, the planned seals—had been separately commissioned and budgeted for (Fgs. 9-13).[65] Extra rent had also to be paid (M. 500 per year)

Fig. 9 Underground hall of columns in the Stuttgart branch house.

Fig. 10 Ceiling painting of the hall of columns, symbol of St Matthew.

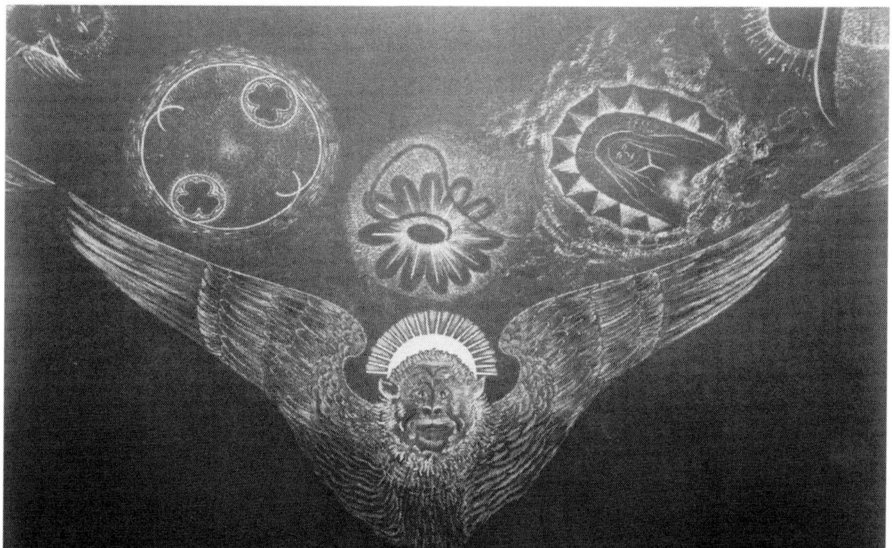

Fig. 11 Ceiling painting of the hall of columns, symbol of St Mark.

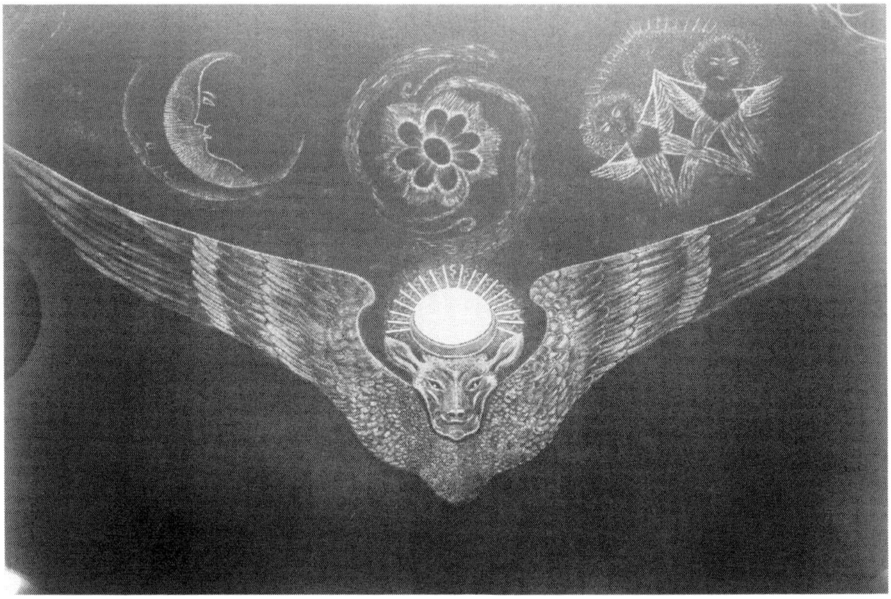

Fig. 12 Ceiling painting of the hall of columns, symbol of St Luke.

Fig. 13 Ceiling painting of the hall of columns, symbol of St John.

for this 'room', and it too had a special dedication six weeks after the official opening. But the official documents say nothing about this.

What is the significance of this 'secret' underground room? On the official dedication day, Steiner refers to it at the end of his talk when he emphasizes the enclosed nature of this place of work in which the seeds of a future spiritual life may quietly open like seeds in the bosom of the earth; and 'only then can they be effectively carried out into the full sunlight of life.' This image is also more suited to the hidden underground room than to the light-filled upper hall.

At the dedication of this lower space on 27 November 1911—the cupola of which had in the meantime been painted by Imme von Eckardstein with very similar motifs to those she had created following indications from Steiner for the Soul Calendar that was in preparation (zodiac, evangelist symbols, staff of Mercury) (Fgs. 10-14)—there was a ceremonial announcement at the end concerning the founding of a 'Society for Theosophical Art'.[66] The small group of people who were there did not know what to make of this, so, on 12 December at the general assembly of the Johannes-Bau Verein (Johannes Building Association) in Berlin, Steiner repeated the announcement. And again there was no echo. The call met souls who had not been prepared for it, and because those whom Steiner had expected to grasp the challenge did not do so, and did not understand it, nothing came of it.

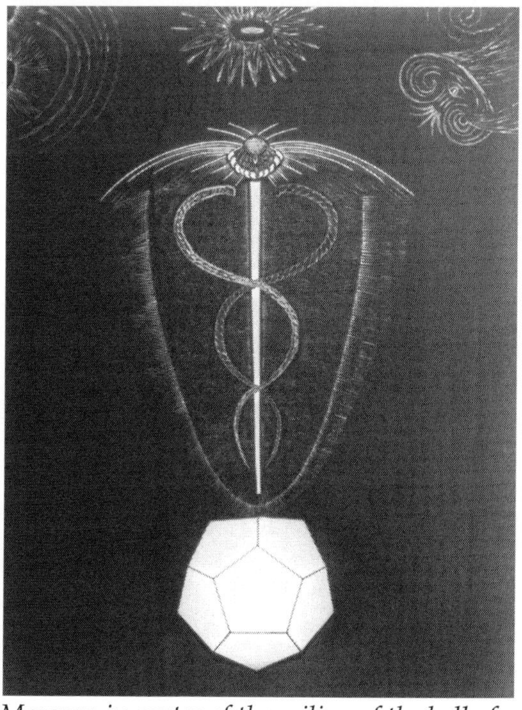

Fig. 14 Staff of Mercury in centre of the ceiling of the hall of columns.

The Munich Building Initiative and the First Goetheanum

While the Stuttgart house was being built, preparations for a large project to build a theatre in Munich were already in progress. At the annual general meetings, Steiner had had one or more mystery drama performed, similar to the Munich Congress of 1907; but it was increasingly felt that the city theatres were not a suitable setting for this content, and so a Johannes Building Association had been set up. Its name derived from the main character of Steiner's first Mystery Drama, and its goal was to build its own theatre. Noticing how serious these intentions were, Steiner decided to put his services entirely at the disposal of this project, and to drive it forward decisively. After the setting up of the Johannes Building Association in Munich in April 1911, he encouraged the drawing up of the first plans, gave indications concerning the foundation stone, and was increasingly engaged the more the building initiative took shape, and finally urged a speedy implementation. Already in August 1911—the second Mystery Drama, 'The Soul's Probation', had just had its first performance—the first plans were presented with the hope of realizing them on a very suitable plot of land in Munich-Schwabing. From this moment onwards Steiner promoted this joint project of the Theosophical Society wherever he went, since the funds could only be raised if the whole society was behind it and really wanted it. And they did want it. Immediately after the annual general meeting in Berlin, the architect commissioned with the job, Carl Schmid-Curtius who had also designed and built the Stuttgart house, began the plans for the 'sacred site' (*Weihestätte*) and submitted them

Fig. 15 The Munich building, spring 1912.

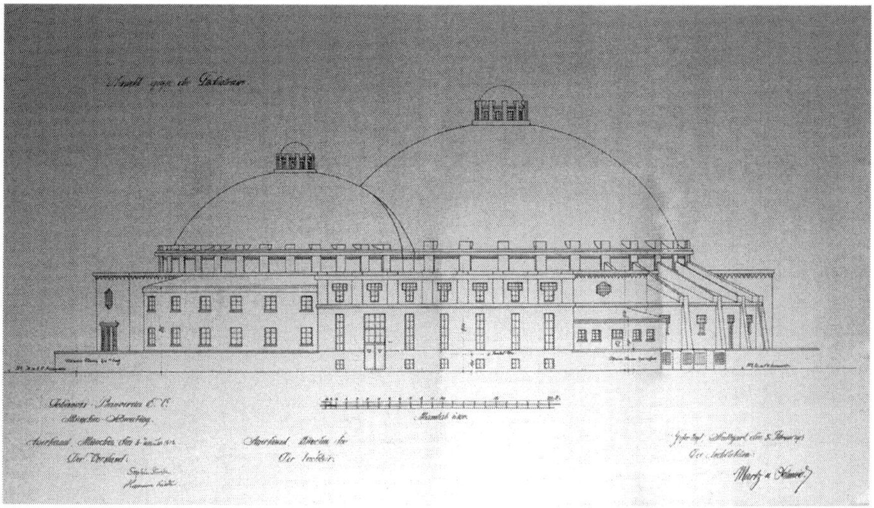

Fig. 16 The Munich building, spring 1912.

to the building authorities (on 7 February 1912). Already at that time the name given to the whole project was 'High School for Spiritual Science', for the intention, alongside the auditorium building, was to build a host of other buildings there, administration buildings, residences, artists' studios, medical practices, and so on. The plot of land which was bought on 8 July 1911, was large enough (8150 m2) to accommodate all of this. The project was approved by the authorities, but was rejected on 29 March 1912 by an 'Arts Commission' convened due to an objection by the Protestant Church authorities, who rightly feared that the project would interfere with the view of the church on the neighbouring plot of land. Unfortunately, the man who designed the church was also a member of the authorizing panel. But they did not give up. The original double cupola—which had been Steiner's idea already in spring 1911—with a tower next to it which was to serve as an administrative centre, was hidden behind a house façade so that it could hardly be seen from outside. This was not so bad, since the main thing was still an underground temple hidden in the ground with no windows facing the surroundings. Only the entrance hall in a representative reception building faced the street. But this design was also rejected by the same commission, and this time clearly on ideological grounds, even though the reason put forward was the 'aesthetic consideration'.[67] (Fig. 18)

In the meantime, Steiner had inspected a site at Dornach near Basel which had been offered, found it suitable, and accepted it. Here there was no arts commission who could impede the builders' artistic intentions, and so the forms that had been found in spirit could be directly implemented. Only now did the plans begin to take shape, and tremendously quickly.

Fig. 17 The Munich building, spring 1912.

Fig. 18 The Munich building, autumn 1912.

In a message on 22 May 1913 to the members of the Anthroposophical Society (by now the German section of the Theosophical Society had been excluded and the Anthroposophical Society founded) Rudolf Steiner himself urged that the building 'under the present circumstances *needs to be built quickly*. My dear friends, I stress the word *quickly* very intentionally.'

The destiny of the building was now such that not only was its site to be Dornach, but the 'temple' was also to be built on a hill. Whereas before it was a case of a more inwardly oriented work of art, it was now important to place the large building in the world in a way that also presented forms outwardly, and united harmoniously with the landscape. In the same way that the temple in Goethe's *Fairy Tale* rises up from its underground existence and appears on the bank of the river, so the 'Goetheanum' will now also appear in the world.

This posed a great challenge for Steiner. Hitherto he had thought about the interior design, initiated plans, and made suggestions. But in Dornach the exterior design was also a consideration, along with the approach routes, viewing spots, and landscaping—for the building would be visible in its surroundings from every direction.

'Creating forms as an expression of inner life' applied in this case not only to the capitals and pedestals of the columns, supplemented by the seven seals (as had been envisioned for Munich), but applied now also to the architraves above the columns, to the motifs above the doors and windows, to the paintings in the larger and smaller cupolas, to the design of the windows, and even to the central sculpture of 'The Group', and so on.

All efforts were now directed towards having one great unified idea running throughout the entire work of art. 'Building a home for anthroposophy,'[68] and finding through spiritual work the appropriate external forms for it, was not so easy. Even the members had to have explained to them why the usual building forms were not suited to anthroposophical spiritual life. Steiner 'made clear that the *artistic forms* for the building had to come out of the same foundation as the *thoughts* of anthroposophy, if it was to be a proper setting for the anthroposophical worldview'. For this, the 'architect' needed to intensify his thinking to such a degree that it becomes a living, mobile thinking that is then inclined out of itself to make a transition into an artistic shaping of forms. Until thinking has developed into an inner perceiving, no outer forms will be found. Because this was the case with Rudolf Steiner,

> it was permissible to represent in artistic form in the Goetheanum what was expressed in its space in forms of knowledge.
>
> What anthroposophy has to represent is the supersensory content of the world in so far as this is accessible to human perception. We feel that every expression of this content through logically structured ideas is only a kind of thought gesture that points us towards this content. And the artistic form appears like other gestures, through which the spiritual world answers the thought gestures; or indeed the other way round, the world reveals the idea as an answer, when one asks it through the artistic image.

Fig. 19 The Goetheanum from the south west.

Fig. 20 The Goetheanum from the west.

> The style of the forms of the Goetheanum could therefore not be naturalistic imitations of any external thing, living or lifeless. Experience of events in the spiritual world is what had to guide our hand, shape our sculptural forms, apply the paint to the surfaces. One had to let the spiritual content of the world flow into linear form, reveal itself in colour.

Once the decision was made to build at Dornach, work began immediately on the models (Figs. 23 and 24), on shaping its forms, and getting everything ready so that the laying of the foundation stone could take place on 20 September 1913. At this deeply moving, ceremonial moment, Rudolf Steiner looks back at historical development, and integrates the building initiative into the development of Christianity.[69] He wished to build a temple that revealed in its structural forms that the human being 'receives the spirit in his soul'[70] and thus makes himself a bearer of the Christ.

In all this effort, it should not be forgotten that the task of building a temple was also comprehensively an artistic task. It was not just a matter of the architectural form; just as important were the sculptural designs and paintings. And because the building was also to serve for the performances of the mysteries, speech needed to be developed as well. And 'because all poetry has a hidden (invisible) eurythmy' behind it,[71] this resulted in the development of eurythmy as an art of movement suffused by a system of laws. 'When this eurythmic art appeared on the Goetheanum stage, one was supposed to have the feeling that the still forms of the interior architecture and its sculpted features related in a completely natural way to the moving human beings. The former were to benevolently take into themselves the latter, as it were. The building and the eurythmic gestures were meant to grow together into a whole.'

Looking back, Rudolf Steiner could even say about this closely related impulse of eurythmic form and architectural form: 'Eurythmy could probably not have been found without the work on the building.'

Despite enormous efforts to build the building *quickly*, there was not enough time to finish it before the outbreak of the First World War. The building association decided on wood as the building material, and Steiner acquiesced to this. It was consequently more time-consuming to carve the individual forms into the wood, so soon dozens of people had to help. Volunteers from many nations rallied together, and it needed Rudolf Steiner's strength to subordinate to shared spiritual goals the nationalism that flared up at that time. When mobilization began after

Fig. 21

the outbreak of the war, many men were called back to their homelands, and as there were now just a few women remaining to do the carving, the building process slowed down. Only towards the end of the war was the Goetheanum sufficiently ready to be used, at least on a provisional basis. Its official opening for this purpose took place on 26 September 1920.

In the months that followed, and despite its unfinished state, the Goetheanum served for the many and various performances, conferences and lectures, until it was burnt down on New Year's Eve 1922/23 by an act of arson. We can only gauge what this event must have meant for the

Fig. 22

Fig. 23 Model of the great cupola hall.

Anthroposophical Society if we are able to imagine how deeply connected the members were with the building! Hundreds of individuals had taken part in the building over longer or shorter periods; they did not only carve and paint, but had also glued planks together, cut window glass, mixed paints, or only helped out with more lowly jobs, in order to build the great work. And now—the product of this shared effort over so many years was reduced in one night to virtually nothing. The pain was enormous. The society was as though in shock, and needed many months before it began to recover from this blow of fate. This time of crises was used by Rudolf Steiner, however, to draw up a new constitution for the Anthroposophical Society which was then actually re-founded during the Christmas Meeting of 1923. In 1924 Steiner worked on a building model which, contrary to the principles that had guided him for the building of the first Goetheanum, developed the enormous structure from its external form.

Fig. 24 Model, view into the smaller cupola space from the larger.

How the interior was to be designed remained open for the time being. Thus the finishings of the interior structure, even of the auditorium, were still uncompleted a few years ago (1996-1998). Due to Steiner's illness and death in March 1925, the shape of the building was only set out in rough outline. It required the full engagement of Steiner's capable students to get the building, at least as an outer structure, so far that by autumn 1928 it could be used provisionally (Figs. 25 and 26). Even today the stage has still not been completed in its final form—a task that may well keep us busy for some years still.

Looking back over the development of the building impulse, it becomes clear that from the Munich Congress (1907) and onwards beyond Steiner's death, the Anthroposophical Society was not only a scientific society but one that included the artistic element within the purview of its tasks. The building impulse had indeed been its centre, but all the other arts had contributed to its completion. A comprehensive work of art was to arise which in all its details wished to make

Fig. 25 The second Goetheanum from the south west.

Fig. 26 The second Goetheanum from the west.

visible the artistic connection, the unity, of anthroposophical spiritual life. From the inner structure of the lectures, to the performances of the Mystery Dramas that included sections of various scenes being done in eurythmy, to the sculptural forms of the architraves and columns, and to the imaginative paintings on both cupolas—everything was integrated into the great idea of evolution. Rudolf Steiner called this the second phase of the Anthroposophical Society's development. It should not be seen as separate from the continuing spiritual-scientific phase, and was still active beyond its high point between 1909 and 1916. This artistic impulse made visible what anthroposophy wanted to say. Now it made its appearance in the world—and on a hill that no-one could miss! The work was no longer done quietly, hidden away and unnoticed; on the contrary, the fate of the Goetheanum was a challenge to world opinion. Because neither of the Goetheanum buildings can be classified according to any ordinary artistic trend, they require even today that we take notice of them and, where possible, engage with them.

Anyone who only knew the 'literary' phase of the Anthroposophical Society could hardly have imagined how all the artistic activities could spring up in so little time. And yet they did! The members really took the artistic impulse to heart; they participated where they could, buckled down to the new tasks, and were whole-heartedly engaged in the beautiful results. But what is the origin of such an impulse, and from where did it draw its energy?

The Inner Aspect of the Building Impulse

Rudolf Steiner's intention 'to create forms as the expression of the inner life,' was formulated in a very specific context which, being one we are generally not familiar with, tends to go unnoticed. The intention comes to light in a letter in which the symbolism of freemasonry is spoken about, and in fact exactly at the point where Steiner writes that he has allowed himself to establish such a group himself. The individual was to move, by a gradual ascent from apprentice to journeyman to master, away from his self-concern (*Selbstbefangenheit*) and participate in wisdom, beauty, and strength, in the masonic work of erecting the temple, which was to be the macrocosmic image of an inner microcosmic soul-wisdom, soul-beauty, and soul-strength.

'The task now,' Steiner continues, 'would be to take hold of masonic life from its externalized forms and give it new birth, whereby the reborn life would also have to bring forth *new* forms. Our ideal should be to create *forms* as an expression of the inner life. For in a time that is unable to behold forms and in beholding to create them, the spirit must of necessity evaporate into a being-less abstraction, and reality must see itself in relation to this merely abstract spirit as a spiritless aggregation of matter.'[72]

The very first artistic formation takes place initially in thinking. As we saw, the German idealists had already noted this. But there are various possibilities for transposing these vivid thought experiences into outer forms, according to the qualities of the art form receiving them. Rudolf Steiner attempted this first of all with the ritual forms of freemasonry. He links up with these forms, which had fulfilled this purpose for centuries, transforms them and thus creates new living images of inner spiritual life.

> Everything that was represented in the content of the 'rituals' that were cultivated in what I had instituted, was done *without a historical reliance* on any tradition. In possession of the formal certificate, *only* such things that arose as a pictorial representation of anthroposophical knowledge were cultivated. And this was done in response to the needs of the members. One strove, together with elaborating the ideas in which spiritual knowledge was given, towards something that speaks directly to people's perception, to people's heart ... Someone entering what I had instituted was told in the clearest way possible that they were not joining an order, but that, as a participant of ceremonial rituals, they would experience a kind of symbolizing, a demonstration of spiritual findings. If there were aspects in these forms which members in traditional orders received or were promoted into higher grades, the purpose was not to be like the traditional orders, but simply to represent in sensory pictures a spiritual ascent in soul-experiences.[73]

Those who were received into this 'class' did not only participate in a figurative ritual performed before them like a piece of theatre, but were themselves part of the ritual, joined the 'acting', had a role themselves in such a ritual. And the ritual itself was derived from real spiritual experience. Accordingly, every participant had his 'role' in his memory, a role that was rooted in a greater framework, and was experienced through active participation. He was supposed to remember and renew this pictorial experience again and again, and live completely within it even outside the actual rituals. As with a meditation, the image developed the energy to think of one's life as permeated by spirit. And an admonishment was added to this: Do not understand with your head the deeply significant image in which you yourself were woven, and into which you should still often be woven in your memory; understand it with your whole being, so that it becomes a part of this your being; so that you can learn to know the feeling that results when you are *completely one* with it and still completely live and weave in it for a while when it has already disappeared from your consciousness. Then the result of the image for you will be to experience what it is to learn to know things, and yourself, and all life, from the viewpoint of the spirit.[74]

The schooling path that was followed in this way served as a special, closed arrangement within the Theosophical Society to deepen anthroposophy. It was one of Steiner's attempts which, as a 'masonic' arrangement, was the least understood from the outside and led to the most vehement attacks against him later on. Seen from inside, however, the opposite was the case. Many members found their spiritual home here and later became involved in the further artistic work as a result of the fruitful experiences they had had here.

At the centre of this masonic world of imagery was the building of the *temple;* not just any kind of external temple, however, but a temple that would allow the working of the spirit to shine out through all its facilities, images and rituals, and at the same time posed a task for the participants: to develop as human beings towards becoming just such a temple of the spirit themselves.

The artistic 'symbolism', in which spiritual content became visible to the eye, was explained down to the smallest detail in special lessons. This was a procedure that did not only contain instruction, but could be remembered later as the images were revealed. All these teachings could be seen as practice in learning to read meaningful forms. Thus, as we know from one of these lessons,[75] an explanation was given for example about the three lamps that burned on each of the altars that faced east, south, and west, connecting them with wisdom, beauty, and strength. And indeed, a burning candle, which consumes its substance and turns it into light that reveals the surroundings, can be used as an image for the development of virtues whose bearers become increasingly pure and selfless, and are more and more there just for what is around them. When Steiner later reveals [76] 'that *the artistic forms* of the building, if it is to be an appropriate setting for the anthroposophical worldview, must come from the same foundation as the *thoughts* of anthroposophy', he means nothing less than what he has already been teaching in the masonic lessons. Nevertheless, the path from the old, traditional symbols to an understanding of every free form is certainly a long one that can only be pursued through untiring inner perception of spiritual processes.

For this new practice it was important for Rudolf Steiner 'that if at all possible, the new should connect with, and carry on from, what is historically there already'.[77] What was historically there already was freemasonry, which, for its part, was very conscious of its connection to the spirituality of the ancient Egyptian. This is not the place to go into the different paths this knowledge has taken through the centuries. Since Goethe's time, however, it has been generally understood that the origins of the Egyptian mysteries are part of freemasonry. We need only think of Mozart's *The Magic Flute*, which was conceived entirely on this understanding.

Steiner also testified to freemasonry's origins in the mysteries, and reiterates this in the lesson he gave during the first annual meeting of the Johannes-Bau Association where the decision was made to build in Munich. From then onwards he no longer wanted this movement to be called 'F.M.' (freemasonry), but the Rite of Misraim. *Misraim* is the Semitic word for Egypt, in both Hebrew and Arabic, and is the name by which Egypt calls itself today.

'What is performed here,' as recalled later by one of the participants in this lesson, 'is an occult service, called the Rite of Misraim, which is as good as saying: the bringing about of a union between the earthly and heavenly elements, the visible and the invisible. The Rite of Misraim was already known in ancient Egypt and was one of the most practised occult rites in the mystery schools. This same rite is now also performed in our temple, with the additions and reforms instituted by Mark. The Mark meant here is the pupil of St Peter, ... who wrote the Gospel According to St Mark when he was bishop of Alexandria in Egypt. Working together with an Egyptian initiate, he gave the occult rite (cultus) a new structure which we know now as the Rite of Misraim.'[78]

When we look at the real mysteries of ancient Egypt, we are led to the beginning of those early ages in which the first, and simultaneously the greatest, building impulse of humanity came to expression, and which shone out as an example for all subsequent impulses: the building of the pyramids. This archetypal temple building arose out of the Hermes mysteries founded by Menes, the whole aim of which was to pour spiritual content into sense-perceptible forms. 'To create forms as the expression of inner life'—this was the creative element of the Egyptian mysteries. In all the buildings, sculptures, paintings, in all the texts and the performance of every rite, we could justifiably ask: what does it mean? And we would receive explanations in abundance, because all the forms were permeated with wisdom. Anyone entering a fully developed Egyptian temple would be instructed, if he had learnt how to 'read', on the structure of the world; anyone able to visit a royal tomb would be instructed on the nature of the human being and his after-death path in the cosmos; in short, all the art of Egypt was drawn from the same spirituality that had revealed itself to the initiates in forms which they beheld.

At the centre of these Hermes mysteries was the knowledge of the nature of the human being himself, with all his sheaths and their various destinies during life and in life after death.[79] The main interest here was the question of the human physical body and its formative forces, how it is a likeness of the cosmos, and how it can be a bearer of the soul and a spirit. As a result of all these questions, what was important for the initiate and his pupils was the polarity in the body's structure that is evident in its differentiation into torso and head. The individually characteristic physiognomy in the head region stood in contrast for him to the torso, governed by its movements together with its organs of metabolism. In accordance with the chief functions of this differentiation, he felt the thinking and perceiving organization of the head to be close to death and the realm of permanence (*djet*), whereas the body's metabolic and limb organization was close to life and the realm of flowing time (*neheh*). Actual life itself played out in rhythmic alternation between these two poles. This double aspect of the human form, which evolves by always mediating between the realm of time and the realm of permanence, found expression symbolically in the staff of Hermes or Mercury, in which two serpents meet each other repeatedly in rhythmic succession. The universally known saying of Hermes Trismegistos—'Everything above is like that which is below; everything below is like that which is above'—also points to this relationship. One of the most impressive images for this double stream of time in its connection with the human being can be seen on the second casket from the grave of Tutankhamun (Fig. 27). There, in encoded hieroglyphics, we read in the lower circle formed by a serpent's body, 'He who causes the flow of time to come into being', and in the upper circle, 'He who destroys the flow of time,'[80] that is, causes it to coagulate into a tableau.

Anyone who has followed Rudolf Steiner's artistic path knows that every station along the way, from the Munich Congress to the building of the second Goetheanum, took place in an awareness of a continuance and re-structuring of the Hermes Mysteries. For this reason, already in Munich, Edouard Schuré's *Drama of Eleusis* is introduced by the figure of Hermes in the following way, and now we can understand why:

(Literal translation)

Think on the seer's word of ancient time:
Arising in the course of time
Is dying for the eternities.
Man fell from divine heights
Into the error and illusion of earth;
But memory of his origin

Fig. 27 Figure on the second casket from the grave of Tutankhamun.

Can give him the being of all truth,
Can form him into a Son of God,
In the earthly body, in existence in time.[81]

In Steiner's first lecture at the Congress,[82] he initially looks back to Egypt and its priests, the servants of Hermes, in order to know at what point of human evolution we find ourselves today. And immediately there come

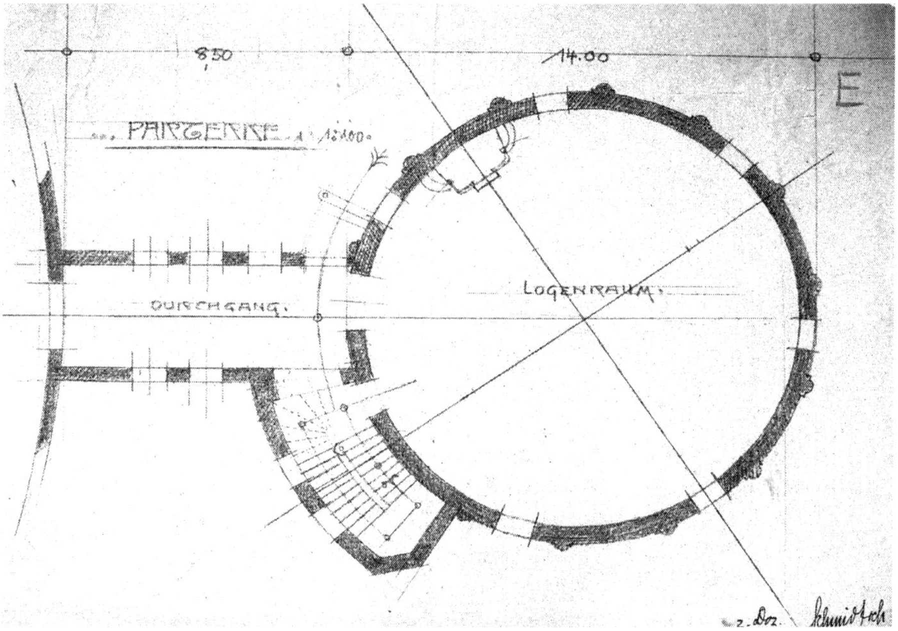

Fig. 28 The 'Lodge Room' in the tower of the Munich building.

the characteristic words, 'Everything below as above, everything above as below,' by which attention is drawn to the important connection for every anthroposophist between spirit and matter. The intention behind the impulse introduced at this congress, was to make it possible for people to gather in buildings in which it is not a matter of indifference what spiritual content they show in their forms! On the contrary, the content of the lectures and meetings should resonate with the design of the whole interior.

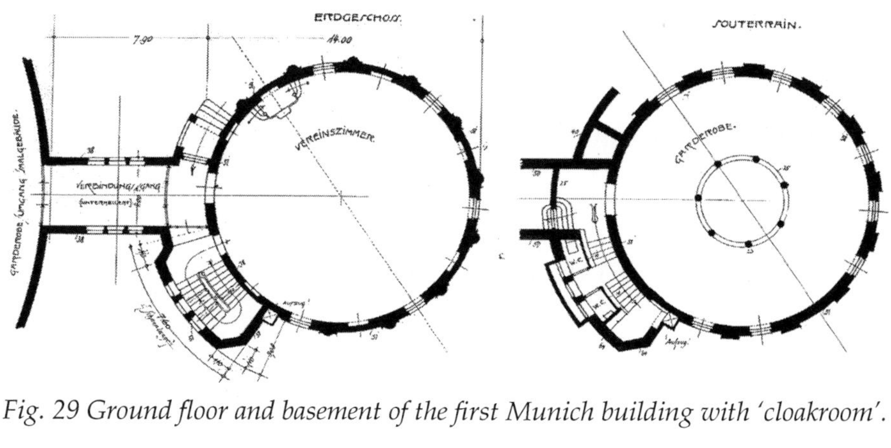

Fig. 29 Ground floor and basement of the first Munich building with 'cloakroom'.

On the foundation stone document of the Malsch building model was also written:

Everything above as below,
Everything below as above.

and then come the two serpents, one light and one dark, each forming a circle.

In Stuttgart there were two rooms at first that were designed according to their function: the large lecture hall above, and the intimate column room in the basement. Down below, the column room was decorated with paintings of the temple that represented an image of the cosmos, with a prominent staff of Mercury at its centre. The hall above still had the sober form of a beautifully wood-panelled room.

Only once the decision had been made to build a shared building in Munich does Rudolf Steiner's plan for a double-domed building appear for the first time, and is then retained for all the Munich projects. This was the first time that the idea arose of a sacred space surrounded by 12 columns, and a more secular space in which the audience sat surrounded by two times seven columns. The architect evidently did not immediately understand the significance of this new form, and his plans show a tower next to the actual 'Johannes Building', with a lodge room accommodated in its cellar, as in Stuttgart (Fig. 28). At first he could not imagine anything other than that an official, public hall was to be

Fig. 30 Final calendar picture of 1912/13. The snake biting its tail.

built, and a more hidden temple room for the Rite of Misraim. This room was labelled 'cloakroom' in the initial plans (Fig. 29), and was only called by its proper function in the private plans. The tower had disappeared in the second design in order to make room for the double-domed idea.

Just how much the idea of this double stream of time governed Rudolf Steiner's work, is evident from the *Soul Calendar* which was created at the same time as the Munich architectural plans. This too is an artistic creation that flows from the same source as both anthroposophy and the building concept for the Goetheanum. Along with the 'decorations' of the signs of the zodiac, the symbols of the four evangelists, the staff of Mercury, and the snake biting its tail—all done by the hand of the same artist (Imme von Eckardstein) who painted the column room in Stuttgart with these same motifs—Steiner wrote a short Foreword in which he explains the intention behind the *Soul Calendar*. It is so that, in the characteristic weekly verses, our 'feeling self-knowledge can experience the cycle of soul life *as timeless, by means of time*.' Once again the double nature of time is evident in time that flows (*neheh*) and the realm of permanence (*djet*). And so that every reader who works with the *Soul Calendar* would notice that Steiner was working here with a renewal of the Egyptian mysteries, he designed the title using hieroglyph-like letters:

Someone able to read hieroglyphics will recognize the Egyptian sign for 'permanence,'  = *djet*, at the beginning of the word, slightly changed, but nevertheless unambiguously legible. How Steiner knew these hieroglyphs remains a mystery. (It is possible he took this picture-letter from the trademark of the Bahlsen company, designed by Heinrich Mittag in 1904, who used this hieroglyph for their *long-lasting* biscuits at the suggestion of the director of the Hanover Museum, Friedrich Tewes.)

Fig. 31 Evangelist symbols and Staff of Mercury from the calendar of 1912/13.

If we look a bit deeper into the Egyptian mysteries which, like all mystery knowledge, could only be attained gradually, we soon discover that the teaching on the 'double nature' of the human form leads to other secrets. The adept was brought to an experience of the time before his birth, and from there he could learn to feel his way backwards to his last death. Once he had reached this point, the teaching of reincarnation of the spirit became actual experience for him, which he could observe in himself. If he reached this stage, he could then pierce beyond it into still earlier pasts of his own evolution, until he reached the beginning of all his incarnations. And finally, the development of humanity, which had taken place in large steps from cultural epoch to epoch, was before him through his own insight.[83]

An individual whose sight had finally advanced this far, was able to discover one of the most remarkable fundamental laws of reincarnation: namely, that his body had this twofold polar structure because, between two incarnations, the forces of the torso metamorphose into those of the head. The movement organization of one life becomes the head organization of the following life![84] An embryo develops from the head downwards, to which a new limb system is then once more attached. We can understand from this transformation how the flowing stream of our actions in time transforms itself and flows into the completed condition of permanence in which everything has become form, i.e. is imprinted into physiognomy. From this point of view, the Hermetic saying:

Everything above as below,
Everything below as above.

holds another, deeper meaning. This background gives Rudolf Steiner's original intention at the Munich Congress of 1907 a different complexion. For, the seed of the building impulse developed out of the seven capitals of the seven columns. Since then there was always the endeavour to follow in thought the sequence of metamorphoses in the capitals from the first to the seventh, and constantly to lead the one over into the other (Figs. 32-43). From time to time someone comes along who believes he has understood the metamorphoses, and can make them comprehensible to others. I myself once had this hope. But anyone trying to be really precise soon notices the deeper problems. If we are honest, we cannot get beyond the fourth capital; the fifth simply cannot be derived from the fourth without contorting it. The problem is resolved, however, when we take into account that each capital has an upper and a lower motif—that is, is itself always double. Following Steiner's advice, the later motifs on the pedestals were developed out of the lower part of the capital motifs. If we bear in mind that columns in all ancient architecture were actually

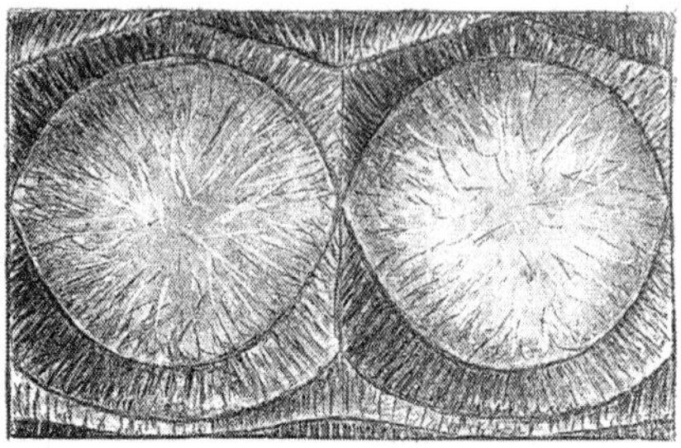

32

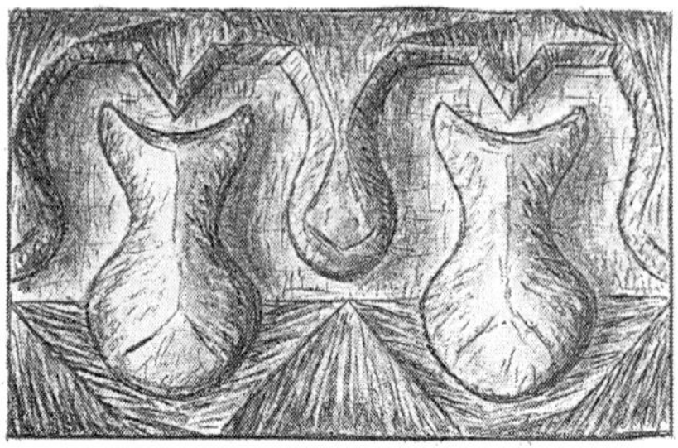

33

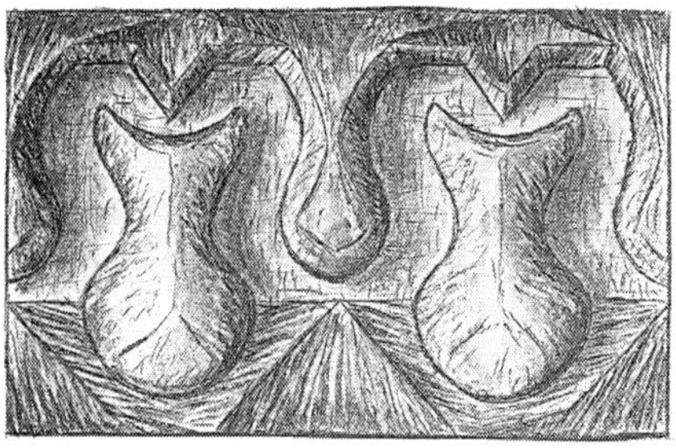

34

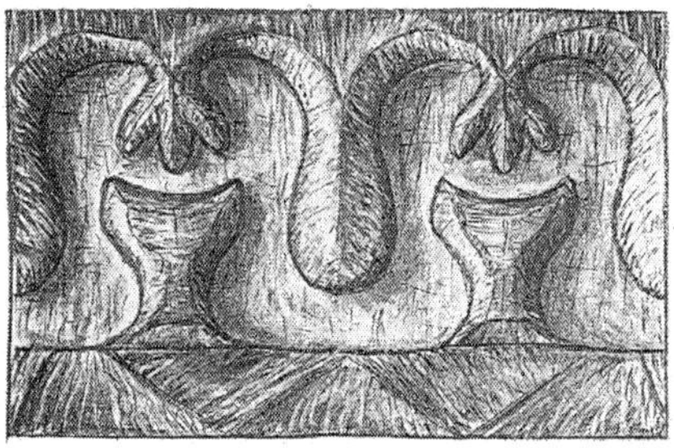

35

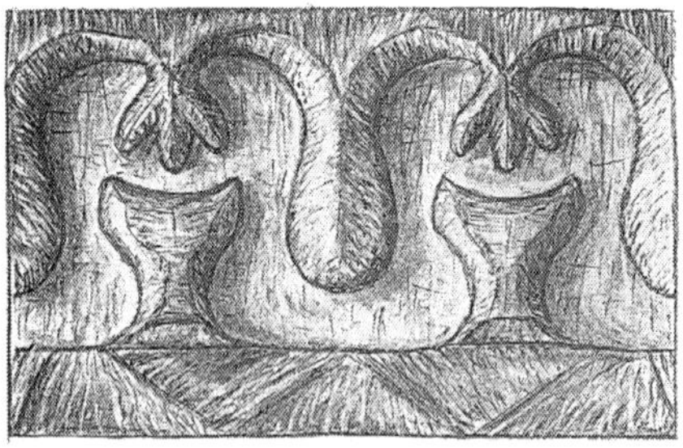

36

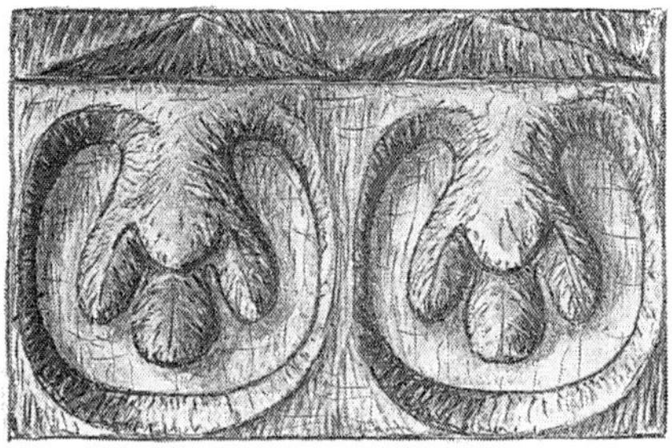

37

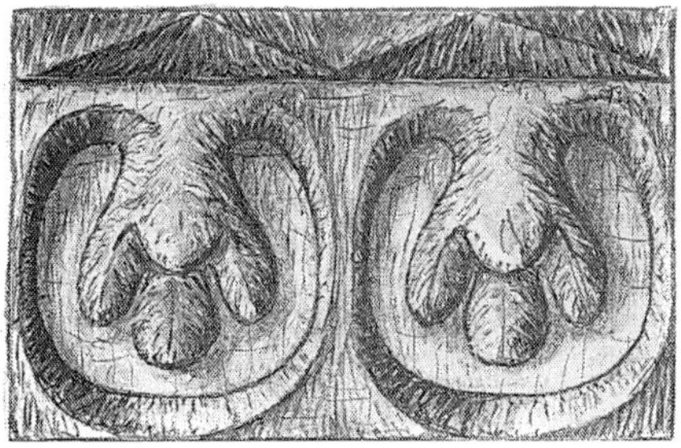

38

39

40

41

42

43

Fig. 32-43 Metamorphosis of the seven capitals (drawings by Axel Schliwa.)

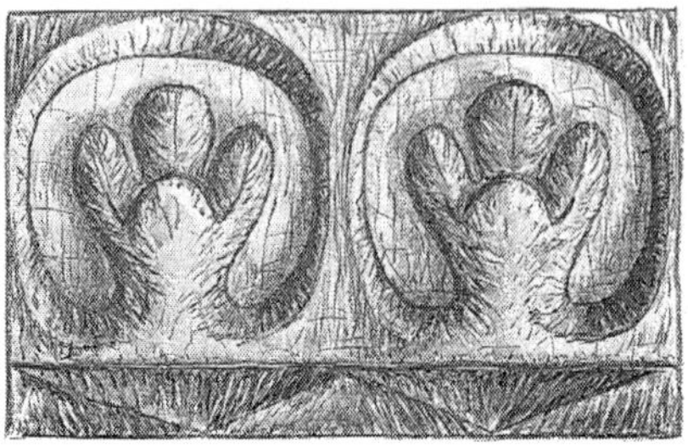

44

45

Fig. 44 and 45 The transition from the fourth to the fifth capital by an inversion of the fourth.

the human being with head (capital) and feet (pedestal), carrying heaven above him, we find again the fundamental underlying idea: namely, everything above as below!

The upper part of the capitals had developed through metamorphosis out of the lower part (which also reverberates in the pedestal)! This can be followed particularly beautifully precisely at the place where we usually fail, and must fail, because the metamorphosis from one station to the next does not run horizontally, but upwards from below, from torso to head (see Figs. 44 and 45)!

The metamorphosis of the body between two incarnations is the basis of human evolution. If the human being were not subject to this, he could not become a free being. Precisely because the capacities and activities of the head are managed with a minimum of metabolism, and are almost purely physical processes that are pictorial [i.e. not directly real] by nature—in seeing as well as in thinking—we are therefore not forced by our consciousness to act. Because of this, the human is a free being.

Here is not the place to go into this peculiarity of the human organism; this was done in detail by Steiner on many occasions.[85] But this difficult idea needs to be touched on here because it is actually the fundamental idea out of which the forms of the Goetheanum arose. The task was to find forms that were the expression of the inner life, forms that represented the supersensory content of the world in so far as this was accessible to human perception. As we saw above, it is from this world that the concept of the Goetheanum building originates, for 'one feels that every expression of this content in logically formed ideas is only a kind of thought-gesture that points towards this content. And the artistic form appears like another gesture, through which the spiritual world answers the thought-gesture; or indeed the other way round: the world reveals the idea as an answer when one asks it through the artistic picture.'[86]

If we ask the changes of form in the seven capitals about their thought content, we get the answer: what is made visible in this sequence of metamorphoses is the fundamental law of the bodily development of the human form, a thought rediscovered by Rudolf Steiner but which had once been the central thought of the Egyptian mysteries.

With this thought in the background, the gradual elaboration of the artistic impulse in general and of the building impulse in particular, from the first seed of the Munich Congress in 1907 to the second Goetheanum, now appears in a completely new light. Now we can also understand why Steiner wanted to connect with the last remnants of the Egyptian mysteries in order to re-found them in a new way, beginning with much-maligned freemasonry, the Rite of Misraim. Yet it is remarkable that every participant in the Rite of Misraim was aware of the fact that the whole ritual could be traced back to the Hermes-mysteries of Egypt, and yet the temple they were planning to build was not compared to an Egyptian temple but to the Temple of Solomon. Again and again in the lessons and wherever such rituals took place, the Temple Legend was told and its wealth of paintings explained. The link was made again and again to Solomon and his famous master of works, Hiram, in order to make clear one's own task through this example. There is an apparent resonance here between the idea of a connection with Christianity and with the Christian masonic tradition, because when Steiner describes the nature of the Temple of Solomon we can always also imagine an Egyptian temple. And it is also likely that the temple building of Egypt had a strong influence on the form of Solomon's Temple. Here we need only mention the open forecourts and the dark holy of holies in which the god wished to live. We can imagine an Egyptian structure from the description of Solomon's Temple, particularly when its wealth of paintings is emphasized, and perhaps even more easily than we presently imagine the structure of the first temple in Jerusalem. Rudolf Steiner emphasizes an aspect of Solomon's Temple that we know little about today, or even nothing at all, because it was completely obliterated with the destruction of the temple. He says, for example:

> What gnosis was in wisdom, the Temple of Solomon was in symbolism. The wisdom that was encompassed in Solomon's Temple contained all the secrets of the world in images. The intention was that those who entered the temple, in which they were surrounded by images that were then reflected in their soul, absorbed something into their soul through which they became human for the first time in the true sense. The Temple of Solomon was to pour the meaning of the world into the soul of those permitted to enter it.[87]

It is not difficult to imagine from this that the members of the Rite of Misraim not only had the wish to advance the building of the temple spiritually [in themselves], but also had a growing wish to establish it as a fact in the world. The Stuttgart Building Association is a good example of this; all its members belonged to the F.M. group, and as a result became actively engaged in the Stuttgart building project. They wanted to build a temple, and turned this aim into deeds.

Thus was built the first branch building of the Theosophical Society in Germany, a house for work with its own temple room for the Rite of Misraim. This fact was specially mentioned by Steiner at the opening ceremony on 15 October 1911. Steiner expressed thanks in general, as we saw above, for the sacrifices and dedicated work that had been done, and then calls to mind the more specific 'work that had to be done particularly in the last years. Recall the moment when, nine and a half months ago, we laid the foundation stone for this building, and consider the willing sacrifice that went into the work that had to precede it. Consider too everything that had to happen through our Stuttgart friends, through the smaller Association which today has taken on the power of the keys to this building, so that we can be united in this new theosophical building.'[88]

A little later in the same speech Steiner again emphasizes the following: 'The work we stand before today, is in the fullest sense a wonderful justification of the trust we had in the faithful labours of the small Association that was at work here. With full understanding and trust, we express our thanks for the exemplary work of this Building Association.'

The small building Association wanted to build a Solomonic Temple. Rudolf Steiner then addresses this intention in the actual dedication, and speaks a text he had taken entirely from the Old Testament:

> O Spirit of the Universe, You who proclaim Yourself to our true self-awareness (*Selbsterkenntnis*), You have graciously received the word which You gave us, in that You saw our work as carried out by Your servants over years; and it becomes manifest today at this hour. The widest spaces of the spirit cannot encompass You, great Spirit of the Universe, Who penetrate with Your thoughts all Your works, and Who wish to live in the words that our lips intone; so how much less can the walls hold You of this temple that we have built to You ...

These highly remarkable words can only be understood when we consider that they were directed specifically to the small Building Association which had made a transition from the powerful experience of artistic images to artistic forms in the world. Just how strongly it was connected with the artistic impulse becomes evident in that, at the dedication of the column room on 27 November 1911—so around six weeks after the opening of the whole house—Steiner expresses a wish to establish a 'society for theosophical art', which, working independently, would take care of developing the fundamental idea further. A few weeks later, on the occasion of the first Annual General Meeting of the Johannes-Bau Association in Berlin, during which the Rite of Misraim was also celebrated and a lesson took place, he repeated this wish, but without the participants understanding what was meant. People stayed with their personal impulses and did not form a goal-oriented society.[89]

Another aspect of special significance regarding Solomon's Temple, and why a building of this kind was so important for Steiner, was revealed only later in lectures that look back again at freemasonry. He says there:

> If one had asked one of the ancient initiates, who knew all about Solomon's Temple, why the temple had been built, the answer would have been something like this: So that there is a sign on the earth that the powers can gaze at who guide souls seeking their way into earthly bodies. Let us understand this properly. Consider that these ancient initiates of Solomon's Temple knew that if they guided human beings into earthly bodies according to all the star signs, then particular souls must be led to the bodies that are in a position to receive reflected in themselves the great symbols of the Temple of Solomon.
>
> Naturally this was a cause to fall into arrogance. If this was not received with humility, with Essene humility, it was a cause to fall into Pharisee wisdom! But the situation was this: The earthly eye looks up to the sky and sees stars. The spiritual eyes of those who led souls from cosmic expanses onto the earth, looked down and saw Solomon's Temple with its symbols. It was a star for them, through whose light they could lead souls into the kind of bodies that would be able to absorb the meaning of Solomon's Temple. It was the central star of the earth, which shone out particularly, into spiritual heights.[90]

It becomes clear from this why the Egyptian mysteries were concerned with the 'Hermes mysteries' or 'the mysteries of birth'.[91] In all antiquity Hermes is known as the soul guide, and indeed not only after death where he led souls into the spiritual fields, but also of birth, where he leads souls down to earth, to a particular nation and a suitable family.

The 'spiritual eyes' of the beings who lead souls out of cosmic expanses to the earth, looked with pleasure at the spiritual content that was 'informed' into artistic formations. These could be buildings or paintings, but also rites and rituals, as long as the forms brought inner, spiritual life to expression.

If we bring to mind the masonic background of the artistic impulse in the anthroposophical movement, we can begin to understand a number of peculiarities in the external development of this impulse. This starts with the Munich Congress of 1907 with its columns and seals, whose motifs follow the great cultural epochs of humanity. The two columns on the stage point unmistakably to Solomon's Temple, as do the signs of the zodiac on the council's table. The words of Hermes in Schuré's drama and put into rhythmic form by Steiner, the explanatory first lecture in which he speaks about the Egyptian Hermes mysteries and about the Hermetic words 'everything above as below, everything below as above'—wherever we look we find the nature of the Egyptian mysteries shining through. A link was made to them in the hope of renewing them.

The Egyptian impulse also shines in the building model in Malsch, which Rudolf Steiner conceived with a view to a larger work, for the foundation stone document shows two circular snake-dragons biting their tails, just as we saw on Tutankhamun's casket.

In Stuttgart Steiner is also thinking of this connection; in his dedication speech he mentions that, in Stuttgart, Hölderlin wrote '*Hen kai Pan*' in Hegel's family album, which refers to the ancient snake symbol.[92] It was particularly important for him to mention this symbol which was also used by the German idealists. We have already mentioned how closely Stuttgart was connected with the artistic work in the *Soul Calendar*; all the zodiacal images, the evangelist symbols, the Staff of Mercury and the snake biting its tail (Figs. 30 and 31) appear there again.

The greatest metamorphosis in the development of the building impulse takes place between the Stuttgart building and the plans for Munich. For the two rooms—the public lecture hall and the hidden subterranean temple room—are now unified into the double-domed space. From now on the two rooms interpenetrate one another according to the Egyptian concept of a flowing stream of time in an open part of the building in which the two-times-seven columns with metamorphosing capitals are lined up, and a stage area determined by the law of twelve-foldness, of permanence. An extra 'lodge room' is no longer necessary; the building has found its proper form. And this remained the case when, by destiny, the building impulse arrived in Dornach. But now, because the Goetheanum was to be built on a hill, consideration had to be given to the exterior aspect of the building. As in Goethe's *Fairy Tale*, the temple here no longer 'wished' to remain hidden underground but to emerge and ray out into the world. Everyone who saw this building could, and would have to, take a stance towards it. Through this, whether it wanted to or not, the Anthroposophical Society now stepped into public view.

In the interior we now find the matured capital forms and their corresponding pedestal motifs, but also the cupola paintings, conceived on a grand scale, depicting the characteristic cultural epochs and the great strides in world evolution right back to Genesis. The concept of the building, of the evolving human being who goes from incarnation to incarnation, from torso to head, and thus constantly advances, becomes more and more evident, particularly if we connect the cupola painting with the fundamental idea. Below, where the columns stand, the human being incarnates anew from stage to stage; above, in the cupola, the succession of cultural epochs is shown step by step, in which the human being participates in his spiritual development.

Rudolf Steiner once described this process. He said that, even if we were only at the beginning stages of practising what is in *Knowledge of the Higher Words—How is it achieved?*, when we encountered another human being, something would jump out from his head like the thought of his previous incarnation.

> If you follow this up, watch how he places his foot, how he swings his arms, or have him before you and observe the gestures he makes with his arms and hands, you get a feeling for the formations he will have in his next incarnation ... If, for example, you are a phrenologist, a cranium researcher, not in a bookish way but from experienced insight, what you are investigating in the cranium is actually the forms of the previous incarnation! ... We must acquire, as it were...such a strong interest in the human being that we get a feeling, which jumps right out at us from his cranium, for his previous incarnation, because... with regard to the physiognomy and shape of the head, the cranium is the transformed human being from his previous incarnation... Thus we reach a perception that does not stop at one form, but advances from form to form, is aware of the changing forms. I have tried to give you a feeling for this shifting of forms by trying myself to fix these transformations in our wooden architecture, in the transition from one capital to the next and the next ... where everything is structured according to the principle of metamorphosis. So that someone who once sees our sequence of columns and everything that goes with it here in our Goetheanum, will get an idea of how flexible our inner soul-attitude needs to be with regard to the outer world.[93]

If we bring to mind today the situation of someone looking at the great auditorium of the first Goetheanum, we can perhaps get an inkling as to why people at that time were so deeply moved by the harmony of the forms. For someone who had done the preparation, who had already learnt to meditate in images, this building was not unfamiliar; on the contrary, he felt at home here and became receptive to the karmic consequences of past earthly lives that came unconsciously to expression in him. Everything that came towards him there from anthroposophy was embedded in the greater interconnections of all world development. The Goetheanum was to have been a building in which anthroposophy could have been cultivated in a very particular way: it would have had the potential to train people in 'karmic vision'. This was the noblest task that Rudolf Steiner had intended for this work, which is also why the pain at the loss of it was so great. 'But the enemies of what must enter modern civilization naturally wanted that what in a real and true sense brings the human being forward, what is necessary for civilization, should be burnt down. And thus it is possible to look into the deeper connections here as well. But let us hope that on the same spot in the near future, forms that awaken vision of karma will again stand before us.'[94]

Many despairing remarks by Steiner make clear how difficult it is to understand a statement like this. How, if they had not yet practised seeing forms as thoughts, could people 'see' that this building held an 'open secret'?

> The building was closed to no-one. It was accessible to all, and basically anyone could have the opportunity to see it. But by far the greatest majority of people saw absolutely nothing. The greatest majority of people saw neither what had been built nor what the building represented. The greatest majority of people stood—to use a Goethean term—before an open secret... The intention was to have a statue as the centre point of the building. This statue represented a group of beings: the Representative of Man, then the Luciferic and Ahrimanic principles. People looked at the statue and, in the age of deeply founded science,...did not know that this statue, fundamentally, is only the veil for an invisible statue. But people did not notice the invisible statue, for this invisible statue was the new Isis, the Isis of a new age.[95]

This remark by Steiner is as clear as it is critical. For, his despair over the lack of understanding in 'the greatest majority of people', who only saw the surface and not what was hidden beneath it and from which it sprang, was so great because people did not independently follow the impulse for the renewal of the Egyptian mysteries. People kept asking about the meaning of this or that, without letting themselves be taught by the actual forms. But these are characteristics we all have, which is why the fundamental idea of the whole thing is so hard to find.

It can no longer be ascertained whether Rudolf Steiner knew where his impulse would lead him when, at the Munich Congress in 1907, he referred to their task as an open secret. But, with the building project, he had got involved in a process that finally led him to the basic form of the

Munich building design, which then developed further when it 'wanted' to go to Dornach. The building had a destiny too. Since it behaved like a being—see the writing over the rose window: 'and the building becomes a human being'—it also showed its own intentions. It did not want to be realized in Munich, and its destiny brought about its move to Dornach. Steiner later on often confirmed this working of destiny.

Above and beyond this, we can also have an inkling that perhaps even the fire was part of the building-being's destiny. In order to understand this, we can look at the extreme differences in the processes that gave rise to the two Goetheanum buildings. It is clear straight away that the first building was conceived from its interior, from the columns. Only later, when the building was to be constructed on the hill at Dornach, did it get exterior features and an exterior aspect. The second Goetheanum, by contrast, was not designed outwards from its interior functions—which is what Steiner often presented as the right approach for an organic building style—but from a model of the exterior. After the fire, and after the decision on 1 January 1924 to re-build, Steiner first made a model of the exterior form, and the architects who took over from him had the job of working out how the necessary interior spaces were to be accommodated inside this outer shell. Can we not recognize in this gigantic metamorphosis the well-known law of transformation from torso to head, from the interior columns to the shell of the new building? In order to make the inversion, this transformation must pass through the infinitely distant plane, the form must expand in order to contract once more, exactly as happened with the burning of the first Goetheanum, so as to take shape again in the shell of the second.

Let us summarize: In the second phase of the Anthroposophical Society's development, the artistic impulse is at the forefront of its activities. To be sure, this impulse does not occupy all the members—the new members concentrate on penetrating spiritual science with their thinking—but those who had been there from the beginning now strive to penetrate more deeply with their soul life into anthroposophy. This happens initially by participating in artistically designed rituals in the Rite of Misraim; the building impulse develops from there with the mystery dramas; as a continuation and completion of these come eurythmy and speech formation. The members take an active part in all these activities; they participate in the meaningful images of the masonic cults, take part and assist in the performances of the mystery dramas. And when the building impulse moves to Dornach, they help with the building work, carve the capitals and pedestals, the architraves and wall motifs. If they are inexperienced, they are put to carving the walls; later, those who have the skill paint the cupolas; others train as eurythmists. In short, there were the most diverse possibilities for every member to get involved in the artistic impulse. Henceforward anthroposophy has an effect on the members' lives and becomes something that determines their destiny. The burning down of the first Goetheanum showed clearly how much this connection had increased, for what happened on New Year's Eve of 1922/23 hit the members deeply. People were still involved with it, had donated money, had engaged personally in the shared building work so that they could be exposed again and again to the wonderful forms and participate in anthroposophical 'events'. And now the entire physical-spiritual structure disappeared from outer view overnight. With a single blow the members were deprived of the possibility of learning from forms that awakened vision of karma. This was also a deep obstruction in the development of those who wanted to create such forms. At the beginning there had been the impulse 'to create forms as an expression of inner life'; at the end, with the completion of the spiritual centre, there would have been the potential to fructify the inner life by the impression of the outer form.

The only 'form' that has remained from the first Goetheanum is the group statue of the Representative of Humanity. When the fire broke out it was still incomplete in Rudolf Steiner's studio. It was to have been the focal point, the centre which everyone would see who sat in the great auditorium, their thoughts turned towards anthroposophy. This colossal statue, alone by its size and what radiated from it, was to have made clear that the whole impulse of anthroposophy, and thus also of the whole artistic impulse, was oriented towards this focal point. Only we should not forget here that even this statue consists of a group of figures (Christ, Lucifer, Ahriman, and so on, see Fig. 46) which themselves represent once more the concept of evolution. Overcoming, through the working of Christ, the two powers that threaten the human being from without and from within, and which wish to deflect him from his path of development, is the central thought of anthroposophy. Our future, however, depends on our perceiving this thought and making it our own.

If even just the external sight of the Goetheanum stimulated such thoughts, then this applied to a far greater degree to those who were not yet incarnated. As still-unborn, they look down to the 'star' on earth that shines towards them, that gives them an orientation according to which they would like to align their life. They look down at all the forms of art, at the rituals in which they participate,[96] at the 'temple' with its harmonizing forms and images, and at the eurythmy contributions that could have taken place there. The anthroposophists at that time did not consist only of registered and paid-up members,

Fig. 46 The focal group of the first Goetheanum.

but equally of the hosts of the deceased who felt drawn to the formative thinking, and the hosts of the as-yet-unborn who found an interest in the spiritually permeated forms. (If an aside may be allowed: the external questions about the constitution, as long as work was being done, would have interested no-one, neither the members nor the participating spiritual beings.)

It goes without saying that this so-called second phase of the Anthroposophical Society's development did not come to a stop after around 1916. Today every anthroposophist goes through their second phase, namely when they are themselves ready to participate in artistic works *that wish to bring the spiritual to expression.* It must be emphasized that this is in addition to other things. No particular artistic activity is meant here, but rather any art form that is open to a higher spirituality, for only this attains the intended effect. We could also say that the Society moves from a striving for wisdom to a striving for beauty—the second ideal of masonic work. But this ideal endures, and will continue to endure for as long as there are anthroposophists who pursue it.

The Earth Mysteries and Taking up the Tasks of Civilization

The First World War began in the middle of the building period. Despite Steiner's urging and pushing, it was not possible to get the building finished before the outbreak of the war due to the rejection of the building application in Munich, and the laying of the foundation stone had to be postponed. The male workforce was gradually called up, and fewer and fewer of the able ladies were in a position to finance a year-long stay in Switzerland. Despite the greatest efforts, it was not until 1920 that the Goetheanum could finally be used on a provisional basis. But the world had changed. The greater part of Germany's wealth was gone, the apparent inner consolidation of social norms proved fragile, the old power structures were questioned along with all their associated institutions.

Outwardly it was a chaotic time, but one in which everyone could see that things could not go on in the same old way. New ideas found open ears, people were prepared to experiment with new things. Since Rudolf Steiner was constantly asked about revolutionary ideas, he developed the idea of a threefold social order, and people who thought they had understood the idea, spread it about with much propaganda. Groups were formed, periodicals set up, leaflets printed, works' meetings held, lectures announced; and many anthroposophists took the opportunity to act for their particular concern. As always in such cases, the start seemed easy, but maintaining it and staying constantly engaged was difficult. Many also withdrew and left the field to others who could then not manage the alarming increase in work.

In this fertile chaos came the founding of the Waldorf School in Stuttgart in 1919, the steadiest rock in the current, primarily because Steiner remained warmly connected with it and made a personal commitment to it. All the other enterprises—the merger of operations in 'Kommender Tag', the associated publisher, the laboratories, social initiatives etc.—had all been liquidated by 1923. It was naturally difficult to pull through economically in a time of hyperinflation, but the external factors were not the only ones responsible for the failures. The Goetheanum burnt down just as the difficulties were reaching a climax, thus showing in an external picture the inner condition of the Society. In such a case it goes without saying that the internal peace within the Anthroposophical Society was also gone; mutual accusations flew everywhere, people were no longer recognized in their work, and thus many contributed with passionate emotions to the further disruption of the Society.

Initially Rudolf Steiner could think of no other way to help than by trying to make people conscious of what was living beneath the surface of it all, but without any immediate healing effect. People were distraught; as always in such cases, they looked for blame in others, and were under the impression that they had made themselves available for the various undertakings out of the purest of motives. The young people particularly, who had come back from the war, wanted to do everything differently, even when they had not yet developed the capacities to do so. The older members on the other hand had worked their way deeply into spiritual science over many years; they certainly knew a great deal, but also considered they knew the reasons why things could not succeed when people engaged in outer action.

In this situation Steiner had even advised the forming of two societies, one that could move forward much in the style of the 'old' Anthroposophical Society, and one in which the younger members could feel at home. Later, when the younger people had gained some awareness, they could no longer see why their own society, the 'Free Anthroposophical Society', had been established, and so the two groups joined together again.

Since the other European countries were not so entangled in this untenable situation because the members there had not founded their own organizations, it was easier to get them to found their own national societies which, it was hoped, would then combine into a single international Anthroposophical Society. Thus in 1923 Rudolf Steiner travelled to various European countries in order to found a 'national society' on home ground there. The intention was that, at Christmas 1923, the International Anthroposophical Society would be formed by combining all the national societies.

We can well imagine that throughout the year of 1923 Steiner did not particularly look forward to working for the Anthroposophical Society, for the original warm relationship that had been evident in Stuttgart in 1910/11 had completely cooled down. To be sure, there were still individual members who were highly valued by him, but when they became involved in the executive committees or in any other organization, the cohesion went into abeyance fairly quickly. Steiner complained again and again about people's decreasing interest in the Anthroposophical Society in favour of their own initiatives or their own areas of work. People only had the 'daughters' in their consciousness and forgot the 'mother', who in the final analysis had made all the other projects possible.

Up to now Steiner had seen it as his task to develop and extend anthroposophy, to get the artistic impulse on its legs, and to help in an advisory capacity when people needed him in the many practical areas. He developed a pedagogy for the Waldorf School, visited its teachers' meetings, occupied himself with medicine and discovered remedies; he gave advice and the preparations for agriculture, and helped to found the Christian Community. But he left the running of the Anthroposophical Society in the hands of the elected executive committees. This all went well for as long as the executive committees did not have to be responsible for the outward actions of the members in the culture at large. But the moment an anthroposophist professed to be working out of anthroposophy, for example as a teacher in a Waldorf school, what he did was no longer attributed to him alone but to anthroposophy. Because of individual ineptitude, a host of opponents arose against the Anthroposophical Society, often only because what was done went against the usual schemata. Because Rudolf Steiner always respected individual freedom, he had always emphasized, even in the chaos of 1923, that:

> It is never my intention in my lectures to go into the developmental situation, the organization and the like of the Anthroposophical Society, since I have to see it as my task to work for anthroposophy itself, and am happy to leave the discussions and factors for the Society's development to others who have in various places taken on the running of the Society.[97]

So people were highly surprised when, at the end of the same year, at the beginning of the Christmas Conference, they heard Steiner say:

> So, what should be the actual starting point of this Christmas Conference, and what do the experiences of the last ten years in which the Anthroposophical Society has existed, teach us? ... I had good reasons in 1912, 1913 when I said that the Anthroposophical Society as such must now lead itself, must now run itself, and that I had to withdraw to the position of an advisor who did not intervene directly in the operations. Now, the situation today is that over the past few weeks, after a difficult inner struggle, it has become clear to me that it would be impossible for me to continue to lead the anthroposophist movement within the Anthroposophical Society if this Christmas Conference did not agree to me taking on in all its forms the leadership and chair of the Anthroposophical Society that is to be founded here in Dornach at the Goetheanum.[98]

A preliminary question would be to ask what had happened in Rudolf Steiner's life to cause this turnaround? For in all the negotiations that had taken place to try to get out of the chaotic situation, there was no obvious factor that could lead a participant to such a perspective of the future. On the contrary, Steiner expressed on numerous occasions his inclination to withdraw, a situation which would have enabled him to carry on peacefully with his anthroposophical research without being constantly drawn into human disputes. Steiner went gladly to places where competent work was going on, such as the Waldorf school where he discussed individual cases with the teachers, helped in working out the curriculum, trained the teachers in Waldorf pedagogy, and so on. But the endless meetings that were necessary in order to clarify the tasks of an Anthroposophical Society and to hold people's various personal ambitions in check, were a horror for him. And now the decision to involve himself completely in precisely this society, to take the administration into his own hands and 'to take on the leadership in all its forms'! What could have brought about this change?

Anyone who looks at the year 1923 in Steiner's life can recognize without much difficulty that the journey to England in August has to be taken far more seriously than would be the case for any other lecture tour. There are many signs that point to special experiences that subsequently remained shining in the consciousness of Rudolf Steiner's life path. This is already evident in the preparation for the journey. Daniel Nicol Dunlop, who invited Steiner to Penmaenmawr, a small town on the north coast of Wales, had met him a year earlier in Oxford—a meeting that had a deep recognition behind it. Rudolf Steiner could look forward to seeing him again. Apart from this, Dunlop had already for many years organized so-called 'summer schools' for the Theosophical and now for the Anthroposophical Society, that always took place at special and beautiful locations. In 1922, immediately after having met Steiner, Dunlop offered him a place that Dunlop held to be 'holy', namely Penmaenmawr, where he wished words to be spoken that came from the centre of anthroposophy. Steiner was also looking forward to this.

The tour began in Ilkley (5-17 August) in the north of England's central industrial area, where the land goes over once more into open nature and urban sprawl stops. Steiner was to give a detailed course on Waldorf pedagogy there, which many interested people had come for. People were interested in the new pedagogy and sufficiently open-minded to absorb the anthroposophy that went with it.[99]

Now, Steiner's destiny had so organized things that in both places where he was to give courses—in Ilkley and Penmaenmawr—there were ancient remains of a megalithic culture. This had been unknown to Steiner up to this point; he knew about it neither from books—for at that time it was included in general 'pre-history'—nor from his own supersensory research. Because of the qualities of the geography, which we will discuss later, this had been possible only at these places. To find out what had once occurred there, the ancient sites had to be visited, and this could not happen until the summer of 1923. By 'seeing' these monuments both externally and inwardly, Rudolf Steiner discovered a number of unique characteristics of this ancient cultural stream that were so impressive that he reported on them in many places after his return from England.

If we summarize the most important findings of Rudolf Steiner's research at that time and supplement them with the many scientific observations that have been confirmed since then, we can say the following about megalithic culture:[100]

1. Megalithic people and particularly their priests, the druids, accompanied the life of nature intensively with their feeling during the course of the year. They participated in the shooting growth of plants in the spring, in the ripening of the fruits in summer, and seed-formation in autumn. They felt how the earth closed off from the cosmos during winter, and observed how these rhythmic changes depended on the sun and moon. They built stone instruments (dolmens, stone circles) to enable them to 'penetrate with sight' the interaction of the realms of nature with the forces of the sun and moon during the different seasons of the year. They had an interest in everything that lived and moved, in insects, in fish and birds, and of course in all animals that were under the particular care of people. A beautiful herd of cattle brought more joy to the heart of such a person than his own property, and if the herder could also make beautiful music and sing, he reached the heights of delight. People's skills and energy were particularly valued, so that warriors and acrobats, merchants and seafarers enjoyed the highest regard. It was a culture that was fired by will, by the movements and actions of beings in nature and of human beings. Intellect, by contrast, was less valued, and anyone who withdrew from the world to think and ruminate, had to be cured and made into a useful member of society again. There was no writing and consequently no books. And what use were they anyway since books were only necessary as a stimulus for consciousness?

2. Being tied to bodily processes, the druid priests' faculty for clairvoyant vision of these nature forces was itself subject to daily and seasonal fluctuations.

> This knowledge could be stimulated less strongly at midday. But if the great secrets were to reveal themselves, the priests had to expose

> themselves to these influences during the time that today we call St John's. Then the great wave was attuned to the small waves of his knowledge that adjusted themselves daily. And by experiencing something that he felt—through the effects of the sun that were captured on the earth in this special, artificial way—to be his initiation, his sun initiation, he gained the ability to study and understand the moon forces that were left behind in the earth when the moon had separated from it. This became his knowledge of nature which he attained through the influences of the sun initiation. What revealed itself on the surface of things was not important to him. Through the initiation principle whose traces are preserved today in these monuments, and by the way in which he did what was necessary to gain knowledge, he then saw, when the night sky revealed the stars over the earth and the moon moved through the vault of heaven, what is at work in nature.[101]

With this faculty of sight, the druid sage could not only see the streams of sunlight and of the moon forces in nature, but something more:

> Whereas what I have just described was the case at certain times of the day, we can also say that at other times of the day something else was the case: namely, that streams went back from the earth which could be observed when the sun was not shining on it, and in which were living the moral qualities of the priest's community. So at certain times the priest could see how the moral qualities of his community were [living] in the surroundings. ... Naturally these things are not recorded in what modern science tells us about these sacred sites. But in fact this is what one can see there directly, because the power of the impulses—the impulses of the activity of the druid priests during the times that were propitious for them—because this power was so strong that even today these things still live absolutely in the astral atmosphere there.[102]

3. To his great surprise, because he had never come across anything of this kind before, Rudolf Steiner discovered that the landscape in which the megalithic monuments are found, and especially the sites on which they were erected, have very special qualities. He gives a report on this a few weeks later in Stuttgart: In our anthroposophical circles I have often discussed how

> everything that has to be researched spiritual-scientifically cannot be thought with ordinary thinking but has to be thought in Imaginations. ...We need always to have these Imaginations—not ordinary

> thoughts—in our soul when we describe something directly from spiritual observation. ...But these Imaginations are far more alive than mere abstract thoughts. ... Someone who speaks out of these Imaginations always has them before him as though he were writing. Only he is not writing with the crass abstract letters that our text consists of, but writes in cosmic pictures. In our area here...it is relatively easy...to reach these Imaginations. ...We can say that in regions like our own such Imaginations are relatively easy to write, but they also dissolve just as easily.[103]

In areas like Penmaenmawr and Ilkley, it is certainly more difficult to form Imaginations, one needs to make greater efforts than here, but this difficulty leads on the other hand to making things easier for the spiritual life because:

> once they have been formed, these Imaginations behave as though written into the astral atmosphere; they stay there. One has the feeling everywhere there that if one in some way forms Imaginations that are expressions of the spiritual world, that these remain in the astral atmosphere of that place. And precisely because of this circumstance one is reminded so vividly how the druid priests sought out these special sites, where they were able as though to engrave in an effective way into the astral atmosphere what it was incumbent upon them to form into Imaginations out of cosmic secrets,.[104]

The relationship to the cosmos and to nature did not only affect the individual seers but every person who grew up in the megalithic culture. For the great festivals were celebrated at the time of certain constellations, at the winter and summer solstices and the spring and autumn equinoxes, and on dates dependent on them. People lived in the cycle of the year that is determined by the sun and divided up by the moon. Every living thing senses its dependence on these rhythms, including the human being with his clairvoyant spirit life. The periodic faculty of perception of the druid who was responsible for a particular community and its moral condition, is strangely moving. Steiner had not hitherto known of this because it did not occur in this form in the ancient oriental cultures. Nor was he aware of the strong fluctuations in corporeal clairvoyance which also depended on the sun; for these fluctuations also did not occur in the ancient Orient, probably because the variance in the sun's position during the course of the year is less marked. And finally, the way the formation of imaginative pictures was dependent on the location on earth was also new to Steiner, and an attribute that can only be ascertained by visiting the place oneself.

Surprising though all these research results might be, the consequences of the trip were even more so. In order to get at least an inkling of what happened here, we need to look more closely at the individual monuments visited by Steiner. We can begin with the first stop, with Ilkley.

Ilkley in Yorkshire lies in a gentle valley running east-west. It is bordered to the south by moorland which drops towards the town in two distinct sandstone levels (Fig. 47). Halfway up, at the height of the first level, there are ancient markings at various places engraved in the rock by druid priests. One of these is particularly noticeable and very well-known and shows, on a kind of altar stone on a steep outcrop of rock, a marking of the Guardian of the Threshold, the swastika. It is therefore known as the 'Swastika Stone' (Figs. 48-50). Rudolf Steiner visited this place during his stay. One has to climb through a small forest reserve and then one suddenly comes upon the steep outcrop from which there is a wide view. Steiner stood on the former sacred site and was deeply impressed by it, and mentioned it in the report on the journey which he gave in Dornach after his return:[105]

Fig. 47 The Ilkley landscape.

It is moving when one climbs a hill in this area and then, in the extraordinarily characteristic places, wherever they are, one finds the remains of ancient offering altars with their associated symbols—it is extraordinarily moving. Not far from Ilkley there is just such a hill, on top of this is just such a stone, and on this stone is essentially—it is actually a little bit more complicated—but essentially there is what is called a swastika, which was put into the stones in certain places, was engraved, and which indicates something very special. It indicates how the druid priests were filled at these places with the thoughts which at one time...created the culture in these regions. For if one steps onto a place like this, if one stands in front of such an outcrop of rock with its engraved markings, then one sees even still today the whole situation, that one is standing in the same place where the druid priest once stood, and where he experienced this sign in such a way that he brought the consciousness, which he had from the dignity of his inner stature, to expression in this sign. For, what do we read in this sign when we stand before such a stone? We read the words that were in the heart of the druid priest:

Fig. 48 The Swastika Stone at Ilkley.

Fig. 49 The Swastika Stone from above.

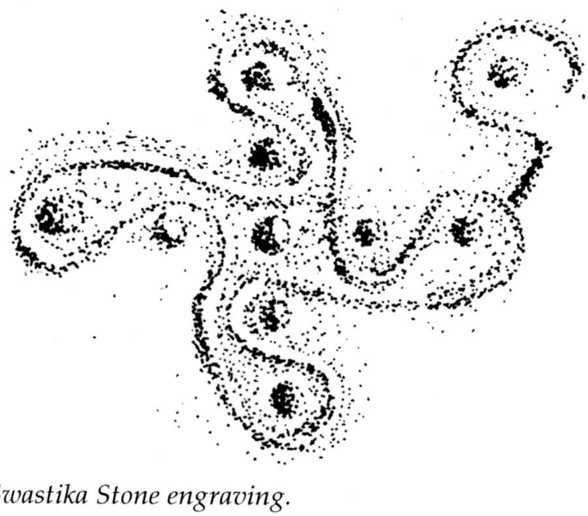

Fig. 50 The Swastika Stone engraving.

> Behold, the sensory eye sees the hills, sees the places of man; the eye of the spirit, the lotus flower, the rotating lotus flower (for the swastika is its symbol) sees into the hearts of human beings, sees into the interior of the soul. And through this seeing I wish to be connected to those who are entrusted to me as my congregation.

This sign must have once been far more impressive than its is today. When it was freshly engraved in the sandstone it must have shone out brightly from the grey weathered surface of the rock. Nowadays it can only be easily seen when the sun is low and shows it in relief. It has lost its former radiance.

From the Swastika Stone the hill climbs steeply to another plateau from which the Ilkley valley is no longer visible. In the middle of this broad, lonely level there is another steep outcrop of rock which again has traces of ancient markings—the second sacred site (Fig. 51). But how different this place is in comparison to the altar stone lower down! One who stands here no longer has any contact with the world of everyday life and its people; it is distant and invisible. But he is closer to the sky and the cosmos. Because of the completely different impression we have in this place, we can assume that the druid priest performed different rituals here from those lower down. Individual stones with 'cup-and-ring marks', which are often found in isolated places, bear witness to this.

The structure of the landscape—the valley with the town of Ilkley, the twofold descent of the sandstone levels to the south—and the location of the monuments, with the Swastika Stone on the edge of the first level and the more distant sacred site higher up from the first, correspond exactly to a sketch drawn by Steiner between 22 and 24 September 1923, a few weeks after his return from England, and which he called 'Druid Stone' (Fig. 52). The picture is structured like the Ilkley landscape, but the colours differ considerably from the natural ones. In the bottom left a massif of rock seems to rise up, drawn in various shadings of blue. On the right is the slope of the north side of the valley, rising more gently than to the south, as a moor-covered ridge. Today the traces of the ancient sacred sites have vanished; markings can no longer be found. Above right shows the radiant sun whose light rays out like a counter-pole to the darkly condensed underground. There are three figures in the blue of the picture, each in a different pose and engaged in different activities. Below right, entirely in the blue and in crystal-like bluish surroundings, is a person sitting on the ground, engaged in some kind of everyday activity. In the centre of the picture

Fig. 51 The upper sacred site over Ilkley moor.

there is a druid priest bowing before his stone altar, from which the sign of the Guardian of the Threshold appears to rotate.[106] He is surrounded by flowing sunlight while he inclines himself towards the world of people down below. Above left there is the upright light-figure of another priest standing in the midst of three altars, as though in a dip in the hillside. He has no connection with the sitting figure down below and is completely dedicated to the upper worlds. There, blue cloud-like formations are floating that part to leave a light cruciform space. At the very top, at the edge of the picture, there are red lines and planes that reach over to the left and even into the darkness of the ground. For the sake of completeness, we can also note the misty brown giant that can be made out in shadowy form on the right edge of the picture.

The posture of each of the three figures is striking: below, the squatting blue figure that barely seems separate from the ground; at the centre, the

Fig. 52 Rudolf Steiner's 'Druid Stone' sketch.

shining figure of the priest officiating at the altar and inclined towards the world and people; and above, the upright, bright spirit-man.

Although the 'Druid Stone' sketch corresponds fairly accurately with the geographical setting at Ilkley, this does not yet tell us anything about the significance of the sketch. On the one hand we need to bear in mind that the impressions from Penmaenmawr are also part [of the drawing], and on the other hand we should not forget that Rudolf Steiner gave this sketch to Ita Wegman, who had participated in the Penmaenmawr course, and who apparently made an important discovery there regarding their joint destiny. Her subsequent question regarding modern mystery-based medicine led to further collaboration in the field of medicine.[107]

Naturally the significance of the sketch is not confined to being an *aide-mémoire* of a beautiful spot, but the identification of the place leads us further. We need only think of what Steiner had observed in these places that were sought out by the druid priests: that the ancient Imaginations were still there. Ilkley was one such place; Steiner was there and experienced that 'the druid priest was filled with the thoughts which had once...shaped the culture in this region'. Steiner was also very moved by the content of [the priest's] vision, which could perceive the soul-condition of the people and wished to be connected with them. But there were also places like this in Penmaenmawr which Steiner visited and where he read what the druid priest had engraved in the astral atmosphere, 'what it was incumbent upon him to form in Imaginations out of the cosmic mysteries'.[108]

If we take these facts seriously, then only a small step will lead us to suspect that the 'Druid Stone' sketch contains one of these enduring Imaginations. A fortnight after he had finished the sketch, Steiner gave five lectures in Dornach with the title '*Das Miterleben des Jahreslaufes in vier kosmischen Imaginationen* (Experiencing the course of the year in four cosmic Imaginations).[109] This, too, was a 'memory' of the summer tour. For it was precisely this experiencing of the course of the year that was the task of the megalithic peoples, and the druid priest had to shape his Imaginations based on the four great festivals, Imaginations that established the connection with the spiritual world. But the Imagination for which the druid priest had to exert all the power he had, when he received 'the great wave' of his visions, was the St John's Imagination—[the time] when the sun was shining with its greatest strength and the greatest festival [of the year] was celebrated. And indeed, the 'Druid Stone' sketch represents nothing less than this Imagination! The festival that is celebrated there was connected with the experience of the spirit in nature, a fact which gave the whole of northern culture its meaning. Following on from this, let us look at the modern 'St John's Imagination'.[110]

Right at the beginning of the lecture Rudolf Steiner describes the human being's feeling at the height of summertime, in which he develops a kind of nature consciousness by inwardly accompanying everything that grows, shoots, and blooms.

'So we can say that during summertime the human being is caught up in nature. But if he has the proper sensibility, the proper feeling for it, then objective spirituality comes to meet him out of weaving nature. So that during St John's Tide the actual human element must be sought in external, objective spirituality. And it is definitely present there in nature.'

Rudolf Steiner turns his perceiving gaze downwards into the depths of the earth and:

> we find there how the rocks in the depths of the earth present us with their inner crystal-forming quality more strongly than at any other season. When we look with imaginative sight into the depths of the earth during St Johns Tide, we have the impression: down there below things live and weave in crystal forms in which the firm earth consolidates itself ... crystal forms that gain their beauty precisely during the time of high summer. ... And if we want an overall impression, then it is this 'being-consolidated-in-itself' of earthly crystalline nature that weaves in dark blue. ... We could put it to be saying that when we send down our gaze we get the impression of linearity, but with everything bathed in blue, and this blue is permeated everywhere by lines with a silvery sheen, so that everywhere in the blue is a silver-glowing, crystallizing element. It is as though nature wants to present us with her formative power in a wonderful sculpture, but a sculpture that we should not see in the way we usually see with our eyes; but rather it is such that we feel ourselves dissolved in this nature sculpture, that we actually feel in ourselves every line that is down there, every silver-glittering line. We feel ourselves as human beings to have formally grown out of the blue underground of the earth, and we feel ourselves inwardly imbued with the energy of the silver-glowing crystal lines [see the blue sitting figure in the sketch]. And when we come back to ourselves and ask, ... 'What is it that is living and weaving in silver-sheen in the earth, in the earthly blue?'—then we know that this is cosmic will. We have the feeling that we are standing on cosmic will ...
>
> When we raise our gaze to the heights, we have the impression of spread-out cosmic intelligence ... there in the heights we have the feeling that weaving intelligence is everywhere; not, however, the weaving intelligence of single beings but of many beings that live together inter-penetrating one another. So above we have the outspread weaving intelligence, through which the light shines—intelligence illuminated and shining, weaving and living (yellow), as the opposite of the will. And while down below we have the feeling that it is blue and dark there, that everything can only be experienced there as forces, we have the feeling up above that everything there is actually such that it enlightens us when we perceive it ... [see the upper forms of the sketch].

> And now a figure appears in this glowing weaving ... Now, in St John's Tide, there comes towards us, if I put it in human terms—the description of everything is naturally only approximate—there immediately comes towards us an exceptionally serious face, an earnest countenance, that rises up warmly glowing as though out of the general shining intelligence [see the suggestion of eyes drawn with red lines at the top of the picture]. We have the impression that this figure forms its light-corporeality out of the shining intelligence.

This figure appearing in the shining intelligence is Uriel. It is that angel of the year's course 'whose own intelligence is, fundamentally, composed of the interaction of the forces of the planets of our planetary system, supported by the influences of the fixed stars of the zodiac' and 'who actually holds cosmic thinking in his own thinking. So that we have the following feeling: You shining, intelligent summer clouds, in which the blue crystal formations of the ground are reflected up above just as the shining, intelligent cloud formations are reflected in turn down below in the crystal formations of the earth, in you, you shining cloud formations, cosmic intellect appears at high summer with earnest countenance, and concentrated into an imagination.' [See the blue cloud formations above, and the earth penetrated by light below right.]

This description is followed by a characterization of the process that takes place between above and below through the deeds of Uriel that are woven in the light. The flashing up of the silver-sheen-element is thereby changed into a golden one. Uriel's gaze is directed towards this process.

> We get the deepest longing to understand this strange gaze of Uriel that is directed downwards. We have the impression that we must find out what this look means. And we get our first insight into what this look signifies when we, as a human being ourself, learn spiritually to look deeper into the blue silver-glowing depths of the earth in summer. Formations that dissolve and then condense again, weave around these silver-glowing crystal rays causing, we could say, a certain interference. ... Now we realize that these...are human errors that are distinct here in their contrast to the regular, internally consistent crystal formations of nature. And it is to this contrast between crystallization in nature with its regular beauty, and the human errors that weave above it, that Uriel's earnest gaze is directed. Here at high summer everything in humankind that is imperfect in contrast to the regular formation of crystal structures, is seen through. It is here that we have the impression from Uriel's earnest gaze that what is in nature is interwoven with morality.

These densifications of error that are mixed in with the regular crystal forms can be easily seen in the sketch. Uriel's gaze is directed to the human being who, piece by piece, transforms the errors and develops virtues:

> Everything that is human virtue, human competence, goes upwards with the silver-glittering lines and appears like the enveloping clouds of Uriel; it enters into the shining intelligence as human virtue transformed into artwork, so to speak, into cloud sculpture. We cannot look up just at this earnest eye in the countenance of Uriel that grows serious due to its gaze into the depths of the earth, without also being able to look up at something there that has what we could describe as wing-like arms or arm-like wings, being Uriel's gesture of earnest admonition which brings what I could call *historical conscience* into humankind. ... Of course you need to picture all this as an Imagination.

If we are aware that an Imagination such as this represents a living picture of a reality, for which the picture is only an expression,

> then the actual St John's Imagination comes towards us. ... Above, the dove, illumined as it were by the energy of Uriel's eye. What is below as the silver-glittering blue condenses into an image; what represents the depths of the earth connected with human incompetence and error, consolidates into the image of the Earth Mother (blue), whether you call her Demeter or Mary. So when we direct our gaze downwards we cannot but take all these secrets of the depths and encapsulate them in an Imagination of that which is the Material-Mother of existence, while we feel in what condenses above, in the flowing figure, everything that is the Spirit-Father of all existence around us. And now we see the result of the working-together of the Spirit-Father and the Material-Mother, something that bears within it in the most beautiful way the harmony between silver Earth-energy and golden Sky-energy—the Son, between Father and Mother. So this Imagination of a trinity arises which is the actual St John's Imagination. The background is creative, seeing, admonishing Uriel.

This trinity consists not of Father, Son, and Spirit but of Spirit-Father, Mother and Son. This feminine trinity deriving from wisdom-filled tradition, was called in Egypt the 'Triad'. It always appears when a process is to be expressed in picture-form that represents the connection between Spirit and Nature. In the sketch, we can see in the form of the blue mountain a sitting figure looking to the right. Above, in the clouds, a bright dove appears to hover, and on the spot where the sign of the Guardian of the Threshold is, Steiner draws, in the blackboard drawing that went with the lecture, a cross in a circle, the Sun-Earth motif. Even the sign of the Guardian of the Threshold represents a rotating cross!

Rudolf Steiner goes on to say that this image actually needs to be transposed into a powerful musical experience as was formerly actually the case in the festival of the megalithic people. 'And it had to sound out in music, because the mystery of the joint existence of man and cosmos at St John's Tide was embodied in this weaving musical sound.' In summing up, reference is made again to the threefoldness as depicted in the sketch: In the Imagination:

> the human being, when he looked up, had to see the world-weaving gold and, taking shape out of the light-radiating gold, the red-warm figure of Uriel ... and Uriel's gaze directed towards the Earth, as I described, and his admonishing gesture. That is the one motif. The human being feels connected with this first motif, which is in the heights, connected with the shining cosmic intelligence. On the other hand, below, he feels connected with what strives for solid form, what is bathed in blue darkness and shines out of a silvery element. Down there below he feels what is the material ground of weaving-living spirit existence. The heights become mysteries, the depths become mysteries, and the human being himself becomes a mystery within cosmic mysteries. The human being feels the crystal-forming force right in his bones. But he also feels how this crystal-forming force that goes right into his bones is in cosmic union with the light-force coming to expression way above in the heights. The human being feels how everything of a moral quality that happens through humankind lives and weaves in these Mysteries of Above, in these Mysteries of Below, and in their union. The human being no longer feels himself separated from the world; he feels himself involved (*hineingestellt*) in the world.

This means that the human being is placed in the world in three different ways, as the sketch also indicates. And to research them, we need to look at 'the Mysteries of the Heights, the Mysteries of the Depths, and the Mysteries of the Middle, or the innermost human being'.

When we realize the precise correspondences between the 'Druid Stone' sketch and the content of the St John's Imagination, it can be quite astonishing; astonishing because it becomes evident that this sketch, which externally seemingly preserves a long-past situation, is inwardly entirely current, and brings before our eyes our present task of recognizing the spirit in nature. But it is astonishing also because Uriel's intention, as described in the St John's Imagination, is precisely to develop our *historical conscience*; this means making people conscious of what point they are actually at in historical evolution. Only when they are aware of this will their present task become clear. Thus the sketch also makes us aware of the historical process, of ancient humanity's connection with the spirit, which was lost in the intervening period, and which today has to be developed once more. But with this—and this is the third surprise—the way is introduced in which this task can be managed: namely by developing our imaginative faculty. And Rudolf Steiner attempts to achieve this in our case through lectures that are themselves Imaginations. If we are able to think our way into them, to participate [inwardly] in constructing them, and to hold them 'livingly' in the pictures as given, we simultaneously school our imaginative ability.

Fig. 53 The two stone circles at Penmaenmawr, centre of picture.

This threefold involvement of what anthroposophy must see as its task with what is represented in the 'Druid Stone' is surely no coincidence. On the contrary, it seems evident from this notable sketch that Steiner saw an inner connection between megalithic culture and anthroposophy, which must have revealed itself to him during his journey. Otherwise he would not only have spoken so often about his discovery of this content, but would also not have organized his lectures so that, without saying so explicitly, what he was speaking about was actually transformed megalithic spiritual life. We have already heard about the lectures on *'Das Miterleben des Jahreslaufes in vier kosmischen Imaginationen'* ('Experiencing the course of the year in four cosmic Imaginations'), but large parts of the Vienna cycle with the title *'Anthroposophie und das menschliche Gemüt'* ('Anthroposophy and the Human Soul'), which are about creating a new Michael festival, derive from the same

Fig. 54 Penmaenmawr, the larger of the two stone circles, facing south-east.

context. Just how deeply Rudolf Steiner was moved in soul and spirit by this culture becomes evident when we read what he says about what he experienced at the ancient Ilkley and Penmaenmawr sites. We have already heard that standing on the ancient altar stone with the engraved swastika had 'something extraordinarily moving' about it. The descriptions of Penmaenmawr are very similar. There are the remains of two stone circles there (Figs. 53-58), on a magical site high above the town and on the edge of a wide moor. He had the following impression there: 'If one had flown up high in an aeroplane, and was so far away that the distance between [the two stone circles] had perhaps disappeared, then looking down one would have in the ground plan of these two stone circles the direct ground plan of what was our Goetheanum.'[111]

Fig. 55 Detail of the larger of the two stone circles, facing south.

Fig. 56 Detail of the larger of the two stone circles, facing north.

Steiner repeats this statement a few days later in Stuttgart: 'These druid circles which we visited—if one had gone up into the air in a balloon and looked down from above on the smaller and the larger circle—they were some way apart, but from a certain height one would not have noticed this distance—one would have seen the two circles as the ground plan of the burnt-down Goetheanum. They are wonderfully situated!'[112]

And Steiner describes this experience a third time, in Vienna: 'On the hill which we climbed there was a larger sun-circle of this kind, and a smaller one a short distance away. If one had gone up in a balloon and looked down on these two druid circles, and ignored the small distance between them, one would have seen—and this was quite gripping—the same ground plan as the Goetheanum had, which was burnt down in Dornach.'[113]

Steiner did not only experience this 'ground plan', he also sent it in this form in a letter from Penmaenmawr to Edith Maryon (see Fig. 59) so that she could make the intended connection herself.[114] Since the external form of the stone circles, which are in fact quite far apart (see Fig. 53), could not have offered any reason for seeing here the ground plan of the first Goetheanum, the 'gripping' quality which Steiner experienced can only have been

Fig. 57 The smaller of the two stone circles, facing south.

Fig. 58 Detail of the smaller of the two stone circles.

Fig. 59 Steiners sketch from his letter to Edith Maryon.

due to an inner accord between the inner ground plan behind the efforts of the megalithic culture, and anthroposophy. This inner accord, which Steiner never spoke about but often hinted at in a veiled way, is what he later drew in the picture that seemed to him to express this appropriately.

Steiner tried to indicate this inner connection already in Ilkley. This can be inferred not only from how much he was moved by what he experienced at the druid altar—this is something that in the whole course of his life did not occur again in this way[115]—but can be deduced from the way in which he reacted to the experience. If we assume that already at Ilkley he was able to read in the astral light the enduring St John's Imagination that had been 'engraved' there with great power by an ancient druid, then he also learnt Uriel's intentions, namely to introduce historic conscience into humanity. Rudolf Steiner responded immediately in an unusual way by interrupting without notice the lecture cycle on Waldorf pedagogy, '*Gegenwärtiges Geisteleben und Erziehung*' (Modern spiritual life and education), and inserted a lecture in which he speaks about the course of humanity from pre-Christian times up to the present. He began the lecture, to his audience's surprise, in the following way:

> Let us use this Sunday lecture, which in its subject matter and content will be dropped from the sequence of pedagogical lectures, in order to look up from earthly human education which we need to acquire as an art, to the great divine educators of all humanity, to the world educators who have led humanity in the course of historical evolution from epoch to epoch, so that in every epoch different things, precisely in a religious and moral context, should be striven for by humanity in connection with world knowledge.[116]

And now, from the perspective of initiation science, the course of human evolution is described as a threefold process in which each step is connected with a corresponding verse of the Rosicrucian saying:

> Ex deo nascimur,
> In Christo morimur,
> Per Spiritum Sanctum reviviscimus.

When we look at the lecture as a whole it becomes evident in succinct form what Rudolf Steiner understood by 'historical conscience'. In the St John's Imagination, for which the Ilkley landscape provided a preliminary external picture, there is the consciousness that Uriel is attempting to bring this historical conscience into mankind, because without it modern humanity will not be able to form an accurate idea of its real tasks. Rudolf Steiner immediately responded to what he experienced at the druid altar, and took up the task.

The connection between Steiner's experiences in Ilkley and Penmaenmawr, and the being of anthroposophy, becomes even clearer when we look at the Christmas Conference itself. Here the Anthroposophical Society was founded in a completely new way. The actual founding was enacted through a spiritual foundation stone in which the Foundation Stone Verse was given to the gathered members at a ceremonial 'consecrated hour'. Henceforward the General Anthroposophical Society was based on the renewal of the ancient mystery saying 'Know Thyself'. This saying is renewed and transformed for the present time insofar as the human soul has to recognize itself now as body, soul, and spirit [literal translation]:

Soul of Man!
You live in the limbs
Which bear you through the world of space
Into the ocean-being of spirit.
Practise *Spirit-remembering*
In depths of soul,
Where in wielding
World-Creator-Existence
Your own I
Comes into being
Within the I of God;
And you will truly *live*
In Human-World-Being.

Soul of Man!
You live in the beat of heart and lung,
That leads you through the rhythm of time
Into your own soul-being's feeling:
Practise *Spirit-contemplation*
In balance of soul,
Where the surging deeds

Of world becoming
Unite
Your own I
With the World-I;
And you will truly *feel*
In Human-Soul-Activity.

Soul of Man!
You live in the resting head,
Which, from the grounds of eternity,
Opens cosmic thoughts to you:
Practise *Spirit-beholding*
In calmness of thought
Where the eternal aims of Gods
Bestow
World-Being-Light
On your own I
For [your] free willing;
And you will truly *think*
In Human-Spirit-Grounds.[117]

This threefold recognition of the human being as body, soul, and spirit now rests on the threefold division of the human being [into head, heart-and-lungs, and limbs]. If we practise this we will truly understand what lies behind the human being. And we will also understand 'the cosmic substance in which the Spirit lives and weaves and works, which streams from the heights and reveals itself in the human head; [and] the Christ-force that is working everywhere in the circumference, weaving in the air, circulating around the Earth, living and operating in our respiratory system; and...forces that rise up out of the depths of the Earth's interior, which operate in our limbs'. It is as though Steiner spoke these words as an explanation of the 'Druid Stone' sketch; for its three figures are placed in the picture in a way that exactly corresponds with the three kinds of mysteries. That Rudolf Steiner was indeed thinking of this background becomes clear to anyone who contemplates the stern words at the end of the 'consecrated hour', for he says:

> The proper ground into which we must lay the present foundation stone, the proper soil is our hearts in their harmonious collaboration, in their goodwill permeated with love, to carry anthroposophical will together through the world. This will ray out to us like a stern

> reminder from the thought-light that can shine out towards us at all times from the dodecahedral Stone of Love that we wish to lower into our hearts today.

What 'will ray out to us like a stern reminder from the thought-light', is known to us from the St John's Imagination as Uriel, 'creating, seeing, admonishing' behind the thought-light.

What lights up and shines behind the spiritual Laying of the Foundation Stone on 25 December 1923, are Rudolf Steiner's experiences in the summer of that year in England. What he perceived at the stone circles, in the high solitude of the Penmaenmawr moorlands, as 'the ground outline of the Goetheanum', appears now, in the two sections of the spiritual Foundation Stone, as the outline of the whole of anthroposophy. For in the same way that the large cupola room, which is dedicated to the idea of human evolution, is placed next to the small cupola room representing this evolution's spiritual foundations, so the practising, threefold human being is placed next to the three Persons of the three-in-one divine Being. Rudolf Steiner added the corresponding sections only at the end of the 'consecrated hour', so that the connection of the human being with the spiritual world only really came to light here. Each of the first verses was thus completed with its spiritual counterpart [literal translation]:

> For the Father-Spirit of the heights holds sway
> In world-depths begetting existence:
> Seraphim, Cherubim, Thrones,
> Let there sound forth from the heights
> What finds its echo in the depths;
> This speaks:
> Ex deo nascimur.
> The elemental spirits hear it
> In the East, West, North, South:
> May human beings hear it.
>
> For the Christ-will holds sway in the circumference
> In cosmic rhythms, blessing souls:
> Kyriotetes, Dynamis, Exusiai,
> Let there be ignited from the East
> What is given form in the West;
> This speaks:
> In Christo morimur.
> The elemental spirits hear it

In the East, West, North, South:
May human beings hear it.

For the Spirit's world-thought holds sway
In world-being, beseeching for light:
Archai, Archangeloi, Angeloi,
Oh may the request from the depths be answered
Which is heard in the heights;
This speaks:
Per Spiritum Sanctum reviviscimus.
The elemental spirits hear it
In the East, West, North, South:
May human beings hear it.

Just how close England was for Steiner here is evident not only from the threefold structure of the St John's Imagination with its two sections, not only in the threefold structure of human evolution as this resounds in the Rosicrucian saying and was represented in Ilkley, but also in the whole situation in which Rudolf Steiner now found himself, which was as though prefigured for him in Ilkley. There Steiner stood, before the ancient sacred stone in which the druid priest had engraved the sign of the Guardian of the Threshold; there he looked back into ancient times in which the druid priest, through his power of vision, was not only connected to the spiritual forces of nature but also to the hearts of the people of his congregation. This had 'something extraordinarily moving' about it. For now, after the Christmas Conference, Rudolf Steiner could also say, in exactly the same way as the druid priest in former times: 'And *I* wish to be connected, through this vision, with those who are entrusted to me as my congregation.' Through the Christmas Conference, Rudolf Steiner did indeed make the sacrifice of taking on the chair of the General Anthroposophical Society with the High School at its centre, and connecting himself with the individuals who took anthroposophy seriously and who wished to follow a spiritual practice in life. What this meant for him, and how hard it was to come to this decision, can be deduced from many of the 'karma lectures' of 1924.

Finally, we can also draw attention to the great lecture cycle that accompanied the whole Christmas Conference in the evenings, '*Die Weltgeschichte in anthroposophischer Beleuchtung*' (World history in the light of anthroposophy).[118] These lectures present in detail what could only be developed in seed form in Ilkley: historic conscience. What Uriel wished to bring into humanity is discussed here by looking at world history not only from the perspective of the evolution of consciousness but also—and this for the first time in the whole of world evolution (!)—by revealing the inner karmic contexts of the individuals who work in shaping this evolution. We become aware—and this is the new aspect within world history—that we were also formerly involved in its decisive steps. Developing historical conscience means recognizing and comprehending one's own karmic involvement with other people and one's own active participation in the process of history.

It follows directly from this that in 1923 Rudolf Steiner as an individual, and also the Anthroposophical Society, were at a turning-point situation in which they had to intervene if anything wholesome was to come out of it. With Steiner, this intervention took the form of taking on the office of leader of the executive committee. Henceforward, however, this office is no longer an ordinary one, for it includes at the same time the far more important task of organizing and leading the High School in which its members can meet one another, and also their leader, in vision (*Schauen*). By means of this vision, Steiner wished to be connected with those who were entrusted to him as a community. And after the events which had preceded the trip to England in 1923, this was no easy decision. But once the Christmas Conference had taken place, and in the months that followed, it nevertheless became clear that many members took the new step enthusiastically and in devoted loyalty, and placed themselves in freedom at the disposal of a joint endeavour. In hindsight, the events during the trip to England, and their hidden significance, were therefore referred to again and again. This is already hinted at in Steiner's valedictory words at Penmaenmawr: 'So I can say that it is my opinion that a tremendous fructification can proceed from this summer school to the whole of the anthroposophical movement.'[119] After returning from the trip, it was said even more clearly: 'The possibility in that place [Penmaenmawr] of merely speaking about anthroposophy ... about the inner aspect of anthroposophy, is something I consider to be one of the most significant chapters in the development of our anthroposophical life.'[120] A few days later, in Stuttgart, and to the surprise of his audience, Steiner wove his experiences in the realm of megalithic culture into the advertised lectures on '*Der Mensch in Vergangentheit, Gegenwart und Zukunft*' (The human being in the past, the present, and the future). He acknowledges this and justifies it like this: 'Why do we pursue these things? ... because, to my feeling, I have to count the course in Penmaenmawr as *indeed one of the most important events* in the history of the anthroposophical movement.'[121] Also after the Christmas Conference, Steiner returns to these experiences again and again, and always when he wants to draw attention to the fact that with the Christmas Conference a turning-point had to come about in the conduct of the members towards the Anthroposophical Society.

Rudolf Steiner was himself very aware of this turning-point. This is expressed most impressively in one of the karma lectures in which Steiner describes the working of karma not only for the ordinary person, rooted in necessity to which free deeds can be added, but also what the working of karma signifies for the initiate. This unique reference deals initially with the ability developed by the initiate to look back into [his] past lives.

> When he looks back into former lives, he knows very well that this or that happened to him. If he had not reached the stage of initiation knowledge, an objective necessity would push him into doing certain things. He would do them inevitably. He would not feel his freedom to be compromised by this because his freedom is in his ordinary consciousness. He does not reach with this [ordinary consciousness] into the region where this necessity operates, just as a fish doesn't come into the open air. But when he has initiation knowledge in himself, then he looks back, sees how things were in a previous life on earth, and regards what he sees there as a task that is apportioned to him for this earth life.[122]

This 'seeing' is nevertheless connected with a loss. Although the initiate knows what his task is, the inner push to get to grips with it is absent, there is no necessity for him any more. There is a danger here of being able to hold back from karmic entanglements if they threaten to become difficult, and not to engage with them. In order to avoid this 'there is only one correction: ... looking back into former lives on earth. There he reads from his karma what the task is for this life. He then does consciously what is incumbent upon him from his former lives. ... He would feel unfree if he could not be in a position to fulfil the task given to him by his former earth lives.'

At this point Steiner adds a very personal remark, which on the surface has nothing to do with the theme under discussion. He says: 'You see, the word *karma* came to Europe via English. People only say "karma" because it is written as *karma*. This pronunciation is incorrect. *Karma* should be pronounced as though it were written with an "ä" [which in English would sound more or less like an "e"]. Since I have been leading the Anthroposophical Society I always say "*Kärma*" [*kerma*].' For Steiner it was not only the word that had come via the English element, but also his karma. And in order to make this clear, he now even says as much! This personal 'parenthesis' would otherwise make no sense, for Steiner knew very well that the word derives from India, and is pronounced there in the same way that he himself had pronounced it for years. Now he wanted gently to show that his karma—that he ought to lead the Anthroposophical Society—came to him via England. He had met it there in an enduring Imagination. This in no way led him to decide on it blindly; on the contrary, he was wrestling with the question even into November 1923—and then came to a free decision!

The process of renewing the ancient mysteries was completed with the Christmas Conference of 1923, but a new element was introduced at the same time. From now on it was clear that intervening in civilization, in other words acting out of anthroposophy, required a continuous schooling, a schooling that could be obtained in the First Class of the also newly founded High School for Spiritual Science. The disorganized actions which people had determined for themselves, and which had led to the chaos of 1922 and 1923, was now transformed into mutual obligations, so that 'the members who wish to be active' could also be aware of their responsibility towards anthroposophy and the Anthroposophical Society. Anyone who wishes to be [outwardly] active, must also consider that the effects will not only be attributed to him personally but to all anthroposophical endeavour. Steiner certainly hoped to have independent co-workers for his goals, but they had to be cognisant of the responsibility they had for the joint endeavour, through their mutual spiritual cohesion. From the Christmas Conference onwards, deciding to become a co-worker was linked with the necessary condition of wishing to remain in harmony with the Anthroposophical Society. On the other hand Rudolf Steiner did all he could to give the co-workers and helpers of a project the spiritual support they needed for the joint work. For example, for as long as he was still able to travel, he visited the college of teachers at the Stuttgart Waldorf School, took part in their meetings, sat in on classes, gave individual and general pedagogical advice, worked on the curriculum; he thus became the obvious spiritual figure with whom the 'Waldorf movement' was identified and recognized.

At the outset of the second phase of the Anthroposophical Society's development was the impulse 'to create forms as an expression of inner life'. The intention now, at the Christmas Conference of 1923, was to reshape the social structure of the members so that beginners in spiritual-scientific work could live alongside those who had represented anthroposophical things for many years. 'What was intended with the Christmas Conference...was to give the Anthroposophical Society a form that is needed in order to cultivate the anthroposophical movement'[123]—this is what was said in the first communication about this event to the members. Here, albeit late but nevertheless clear enough, was what Rudolf Steiner had found in the 'will mysteries' of megalithic culture in England, now renewed in such a way that could be a blessing to the third phase of anthroposophical development. We could say that it was actually now that the third phase began, because in 1916 Steiner was not yet familiar with the third kind of mysteries. These mysteries, due to their special feature of Imaginations that remained in the place where they were formed, and which could only be read there in the akashic chronicle, were completely closed. Anyone wishing to find out about them had to visit the site. And, as Steiner learnt there, anyone who did not know how a community based on spiritual impulses must be formed, could not expect the conditions [to arise] for integrated activity. So between 1918 and 1923 people were more or less left to their own devices, not only because they did not consider a mutual obligation out of a free decision to be necessary, but also because they did not even notice that for an activity to thrive, this is a prerequisite.

In earlier times one was placed by destiny in a certain community, and this affected everything that followed. Today what is important is to decide freely for oneself on a task we recognize to be important, and this then becomes the source of future destiny. The decision to join a destiny-community is not dependent on our background. One of the first to take up this new goal was Ita Wegman during the visit to Penmaenmawr. She made a free decision there to 'participate in the work', and communicated this to Rudolf Steiner who was exceptionally pleased.[124] As a token of his connectedness with her, he then gave her the sketch of the druid stone. (Many elements from a distant past were also playing into this decision, but the decisive point was nevertheless the decision itself.)

Wherever we look when we study the Christmas Conference, the images point again and again to the experiences in England. One of these connections, which makes a deep impression, is very hidden because it is not evident on the surface of the [conference's] content. Up to this time the goal and centre of each phase of anthroposophy's development was the Mystery of Golgotha. The task of the first phase was to bring this into a form that could be *thought* (see page 27 and 36); and the Goetheanum was to present it as an artistic focus that could be *seen*. How does the third phase tie in with this?

In Steiner's final lecture in Penmaenmawr he spoke about the central importance the Mystery of Golgotha had for the development of human freedom. In his retrospect in Dornach on 10 September 1923[125] he even indicates that the region around Penmaenmawr must itself have been of great significance for the development of Christianity in Europe. He must certainly have had this in mind the day before when, in his report on the trip, he thanked Mr Dunlop for the 'spiritually insightful way' in which he had chosen precisely that location. For 'I believe it is important to bear in mind that there are exceptional places of this kind on the earth's surface where, in such a livingly enduring memory, there is directly and livingly present what was once alive there as the Sun-cult which prepared [the way] for the later conversion of North and West Europe to Christianity.'[126]

Anyone reading these words today naturally thinks of the conversion to Christianity through the Teutons and Celts, and all that followed it. But this is expressly not what Steiner meant. This is evident in the final address in Penmaenmawr itself where, looking once more with gratitude at the experiences that had been possible through the landscape, he wonders at the tremendous spiritual intensity of the builders of the monuments. He hopes that this intensity will be inscribed in the hearts of the audience and expand outwards from their hearts.

> For we lived as though in an atmosphere that still radiated something wonderful in these ancient sacred sites. ... It was therefore a good move to choose precisely this place where in a certain sense something could come alive that was once there in Central and Northern Europe before the Mystery of Golgotha moved through the world, something that was waiting for the Mystery of Golgotha but which was not able to continue when Christianity, as I described this morning, came up from the South, something that in a certain sense is still waiting![127]

This spiritual intensity that was once alive there, and actually existed in order to serve the Mystery of Golgotha, is what Rudolf Steiner wished to re-ignite in the hearts of the members through the Christmas Conference, and expand from there. He spoke about this in the 'consecrated hour' and lays the spiritual foundation stone for it. After he had brought the three ancient kinds of mysteries together in a new, re-structured whole, he adds the fourth verse [literal translation*]:

At the turning-point of time
The World-Spirit-Light entered
Into the earthly stream of being;
Night-Darkness
Had held sway;
Day-bright light

---

* Two alternative translations, which take into account the mantric and poetic elements of the Meditation, are to be found in the Appendix, see p. 156.

Rayed into human souls;
Light,
That warms
The hearts of simple shepherds;
Light
That enlightens
The wise heads of kings.

Divine Light,
Christ-Sun,
Warm
Our hearts;
Enlighten
Our heads;
So that [it] may become good
What we
Found from our hearts,
What we,
full of goals, wish to direct
From our heads.

Only now does it become clear that it could not have been ancient Christianity Rudolf Steiner was looking at in Penmaenmawr, but a future Christianity that will evolve for the benefit of humanity when we really act out of the new spiritual knowledge. It is also our task to bring this about.

The Metamorphosis of the Idea of Destiny in Rudolf Steiner's Life

One of the most significant achievements introduced by Rudolf Steiner into the culture of our time is the idea of reincarnation and karma. Prior to this these had been noticed as a phenomenon only in a very preliminary and seminal way. From now on they are something that can not only be thought about but also understood—and this process is continuing. We could say that, among all the other fruitful stimuli given by anthroposophy, a whole new world is opened up here which will be accepted by future humanity as an obvious part of the foundation of its culture.

Initially, the concepts of reincarnation and karma were not present for Steiner either. On the contrary, revolutionary innovations of this kind require a lifetime of work in the realm of thought, a lifetime of observation, and a lifetime of research to gradually reach the results which we can simply 'study'. The basic chapter on this theme in Steiner's book *Theosophy* was revised at least five times, rewritten and extended—no other theme is given such a thorough degree of attention. With hindsight, making destiny comprehensible to thought, and all that this implies, can even be regarded as Rudolf Steiner's true mission. How did this come about?

The situation confronting Steiner at the outset was highly disparate. For although the concept of 'destiny' did indeed exist in German intellectual life, it was understood in many different ways. Religiously-minded people saw it as sent by God, whereas others saw it only as coincidence or chance to be made use of. What was clear, however, was that there were significant events in an individual's life which he did not bring about himself, and had no insight into their origin, which came to meet him from outside, from the world, and determined him. Whether this was really something 'sent' or was just chance, was an open question. For as soon as people began to think about it they quickly noticed that it was not possible to say of a single event or influence whether it would really be significant for them. Only towards the end, when we survey our life as a whole and evaluate the significance of individual events, might we see a significant connection. This was the only situation in which people were prepared to talk about destiny.

For Goethe, who from his own experience regarded the idea of reincarnation as self-evident, the inscrutable consequences of single events posed a problem for a deeper understanding. Despite this, throughout his life he never lost sight of this theme and its complexity. In his book *Wilhelm Meister,* for example, he was constantly giving it new literary form. How far he got in looking at the facts can be seen, for example, in the following conversation[128] where Wilhelm has once again met the valuer for the sale of his father's art collection, and says:

> 'I was very sad at having to sell the gallery, and often missed it later in life. But when I think how it had to be in order to develop a hobby, a talent in me [i.e. of a puppeteer, an actor, and a poet], which would have a far greater effect in my life than those lifeless pictures could ever have done, I am content and honour the destiny that knows how to bring about what is best for me and best for each of us.'
>
> 'Unfortunately I'm once again hearing a young man talk about destiny, who is at an age when one usually tends to ascribe one's lively inclinations to the will of higher beings.'
>
> 'So don't you believe in destiny? In a power that rules over us and guides everything to what is best for us?'
>
> 'It's not a question here of what I believe, nor the place to go into how I try to some extent to clarify for myself the things that are inconceivable for all of us; the question is only, what way of thinking leads to the best for us. The fabric of the world is formed by necessity and chance. Human reason stands between these and knows how to govern them; it treats necessity as the foundation of its existence; it knows how to manage chance, to channel and use it, and only because it stands firm and unshakeable does man deserve to be called a god on the earth. Woe to him who from his youth onwards becomes accustomed to trying to find something arbitrary in necessity, who wants to ascribe a kind of rationality to chance, which can even result in a religion. Is this anything other than renouncing one's own reason and giving free rein to one's inclinations? We imagine we are devout by ambling along without thinking, letting ourselves be determined by pleasant coincidences, and then calling the result of a vacillating life like this, divine guidance.'
>
> 'Were you never in a situation where a small circumstance caused you to take a certain path on which a pleasant opportunity came towards you and then a series of unexpected incidents brought you finally to a goal that you yourself had hardly even thought of? Shouldn't this give us respect for destiny, trust in such a guidance?'

All these questions show in a pleasant literary form the situation that Rudolf Steiner was initially confronted with. Even the great German idealists, who made such tempestuous inroads with regard to thinking and ushered in a new era, held back on this point. None of them dared take on an investigation of destiny, and the reason is understandable. For, until it is possible to follow human beings between their incarnations, any talk of destiny will always remain purely theoretical. The breakthrough for Steiner did also not happen immediately. But when he began to speak about the subject, he had already been researching its foundations for many years.

Steiner's experience of his own destiny was naturally the initial background to all his further research. And this destiny soon became evident. He had barely begun at the Vienna Technical College when he got to know his teacher Karl Julius Schröer, who introduced him to Goethe's *Faust*, which Steiner writes about enthusiastically in his letters. The liking was returned: Schröer also came to value his gifted student, so that he recommended him to Joseph Kürschner who was looking for an editor for Goethe's scientific writings in the context of the *Nationalliteratur* publications. The connection was made, and this led in the end to Steiner having to occupy himself for the next 16 years of this life with Goethe's scientific achievements.

Now, Goethe's scientific writings are precisely that aspect of his works in which he presents his research on the theory of evolution, and which, through him, had found some acceptance in the general culture. Together with associated ideas like metamorphosis, polarity, intensification, etc., there was a wealth of new perspectives that did not only expand the accepted scientific view up to that time, but were thought about in a completely different way. Everything that could be thought in the realm of what is living, in the realm of morphology, in the realm of zoology, and also meteorology, required the involvement of time. Anyone who left this factor out of consideration would be able to understand nothing about evolution. Analytical thinking was of no more use here; to research anything at all that is living, one had to follow processes, have an overview of totalities, and be able to bring both of these together at the same time in one's consciousness.

As we showed in the introductory chapter (see page 13), this was already apparent in the first beginnings of the concept of evolution. Here we will briefly highlight once more that the process that plays out between the *essential nature* and the constantly changing *appearance* [of something] can only be comprehended once we have learnt to follow processes in the world with our thinking, to survey totalities, and keep them present in our consciousness. Neither is possible without practice. This is why Goethe—and the German idealists along with him, who, through mutual exchange [of ideas] and mutual suggestions, participated in the discovery and development of the evolution idea—was so hard to understand, because an unschooled and unpractised thinking can grasp nothing here! Picturing forms in movement and accompanying them with our thinking is not something we have from nature and is not learnt at school; they are capacities that have to be laboriously acquired.

This is not the place to go into this further, and it has already been done elsewhere,[129] but it must be clearly stressed that lively, formative thinking can only arise from practice. Its development requires the free collaboration of the investigator. This was also the case for Rudolf Steiner! He brought with him an innate seed of clairvoyance, and this gift was developed further by lifelong exercises; but his thinking was developed into a living thinking through his study over many years of the works of Goethe and the phenomena they deal with. Thus Rudolf Steiner was not only given a task by destiny but also simultaneously a path of training over many years. This gave him the ability to shape the contents he gained through his clairvoyance into an organic thinking, so that anyone with an interest in these things can learn to comprehend them without himself being clairvoyant.

But the work on Goethe, given to Steiner by destiny, did not only require thinking about Goethe's works, since this in itself could not have resulted in a meaningful commentary on them. Something more was required. This 'more' was a higher understanding of Goethe's way of thinking. For Steiner to be able to write his 'supplement', *Grundlinien einer Erkenntnistheorie der Goetheschen Weltanschauung*[130] (An outline of the theory of knowledge in Goethe's world view), to the Kürschner publication, he had to go beyond Goethe in order to understand him from a higher standpoint. He describes this struggle in *The Course of My Life*,[131] as follows:

> I now had to show that although Goethe could *live* in his soul by advancing cognitively from nature through the senses (*Sinnes-Natur*) to nature through the mind (*Geist-Natur*), anyone else can only fully *comprehend* Goethe's soul-life by going beyond it and himself bringing the findings to a point where they become a perception [or comprehension] of the spiritual world in the form of ideas.
>
> Goethe stood within [the world of] the mind [or spirit] when he spoke about nature. He was afraid of becoming abstract if he were to go further from this 'standing within' to a life of thoughts *about*

> this 'standing within'. He wanted to *feel* himself in spirit, but did not want to *think* himself in spirit.
>
> I often had the sense that I was being untrue to Goethe's way of thinking when I nevertheless presented thoughts *about* his world-view. And in almost every detail that I had to interpret with regard to Goethe, I had again and again to master the method of speaking about Goethe using Goethe's own way of doing things.
>
> My presentation of Goethe's ideas was a struggle over many years to understand Goethe better and better through his own thoughts. When I look back at this struggle, I have to say that I owe it much for the development of my spiritual findings and experiences. My development progressed much more slowly because of it than would have been the case if the Goethe-task had not been placed by destiny in the course of my life. I would then have pursued my spiritual findings and presented them as they came to me. I would have been pulled faster into the spiritual world; but I would have had no reason to go struggling down into my own inner being.

And this passage could be completed by saying that in that case Steiner would also not have been able to present it in a comprehensible way.

Steiner's real teacher was Goethe. Although he did not have Goethe before him as an external pupil would, he was nevertheless strictly taught by him inwardly. Steiner describes this unusual relationship very clearly in *The Course of My Life:*[132]

> During the time when I was working on my interpretation of Goethe's work, I had Goethe constantly at my side like an admonisher who called unceasingly to me: Whoever advances too quickly on spiritual paths can indeed reach a narrowly limited experience of the spirit, but he steps impoverished out of the riches of life into the content of reality.

That this experience is based on an actual event can be deduced from the fact that Goethe once expressed the same thought to Eckermann, but then he was criticizing Aristotle:[133] 'Aristotle, he said, had seen nature better than any modern person, but he was too hasty with his opinions. One must proceed in a slow and relaxed manner with nature if one wants to gain anything from her.'

Rudolf Steiner apparently had by nature the same tendency as Aristotle, and thus Goethe wanted to dissuade him from it. And this he also managed to do!

Later on Steiner was grateful to his destiny for having granted him this education. It gave him the Goethe-task and took him to Weimar. He followed this call but was already wide-awake during this whole period and observed how it came about! In hindsight it became even clearer. Thus he could say of his time in Weimar:[134]

> In my relationship to my Goethe work I could observe very plainly 'how karma operates in human life'. Destiny is a combination of two sets of factors which grow together into a unity in a person's life. The one set streams outwards from the impulses of the soul, and the other comes towards us from the external world. The urge of my own soul was towards perception of the spirit; the external intellectual life of the world brought the Goethe work to me. I had to bring these two streams into harmony, which met in my consciousness.

This particular guidance and task of destiny is naturally connected with Rudolf Steiner's most essential striving, for it arises from how his view of the world and of life developed. In retrospect he even highlights a particular detail which at the time must surely have seemed not at all desirable:[135]

> When I look back at the first part of my life, I have a strong feeling, when I try to characterize it from the outside, that destiny led me in such a way that in my thirtieth year I did not see myself tied to any external 'profession'. Also I did not go to the Goethe and Schiller Archive in Weimar as a job for life, but as a freelance collaborator on the Goethe edition, whose publication by the archive was commissioned by the Grand-Duchess Sophie.

This working in a freelance capacity remained characteristic for the rest of Steiner's life. It allowed him a free and self-determined spiritual life which could unfold independently of external influences.

Steiner was aware early on of the operation of destiny that meets the human being out of the past, but also on the other hand of the response that follows it, independent of any necessity, out of a person's free will. In this sense Goethe's *Fairy Tale* was significant for him, which Goethe wrote in response to Schiller's aesthetic letters. [The *Fairy Tale*] describes in imaginative pictures what constitutes the complicated being of man. This fairy tale now becomes a life-theme for Rudolf Steiner. It begins very quietly, as follows:[136]

> In this fairy tale, Goethe brought imaginative creation close to the borderline where it passes over into the inner soul-process that is a

cognitive experience of the real spiritual worlds. It seemed to me that one could look most deeply into one's heart and mind by pondering this work.

What was important to me from studying the fairy tale was not an explanation [of it] but the stimulus [it gave] for soul experience. This stimulus continued to work on in my subsequent soul-life and right into the shaping of the Mystery Dramas I later wrote. But I could not gain much from the fairy tale for my works which were influenced by Goethe. For it seemed to me that, in writing this tale, Goethe had grown beyond himself in his worldview, as though driven by an inner power of a half unconscious soul-life. And this posed a serious difficulty for me. I could only continue my interpretation of Goethe for Kürschner's *Deutsche Nationalliteratur* in the same style with which I had begun it; but for me something was lacking. For I said to myself that, while he was writing the *Fairy Tale*, Goethe had as though looked beyond the border to the spiritual world and seen into that world. But what he then wrote about processes in nature did not take this impression into account. So one can therefore not interpret him from the standpoint of this insight.

But although I did not initially gain anything for my writing on Goethe by pondering his fairy tale, I nevertheless gained an abundance of stimuli from it for the soul. The soul-content I derived from the fairy tale became an important subject of meditation. I returned to it again and again.

During his Weimar period it was not only the idea of evolution, introduced by Goethe and the German idealists, that matured for Steiner; he also made progress, through his own experience and his own observation, in his understanding of destiny. Finally, also through steady meditation on the fairy tale, he continued to shape his view of man's being, including all the forces that have flowed into humanity through the Mystery of Golgotha. All this was living in his mind when he moved to Berlin in order to take up the editorship of the *Magazin für Literatur* (Magazine for literature). But here too he did not find the people he was longing for, who had an interest in a higher understanding of the human being and the world. The wish to publicly present the esoteric things that were living in him, drove him, on the occasion of Goethe's 150th birthday, to write an article in the magazine with the title 'Goethe's Secret Revelation'. Although he managed to give this article an 'esoteric mood', he was still unable to speak about what was really moving him inwardly. The first time this occurred was when he was asked by Count and Countess Brockdorff to give a lecture on Nietzsche, on which occasion he noticed that there were individuals among the audience with a great interest in the spiritual world. When he was asked to give a second lecture, he suggested he speak about 'Goethe's secret revelation'. 'And in *this* lecture, in connection with the *Fairy Tale*, I spoke completely esoterically. It was an important experience for me, to be able to speak words that were formed out of the spirit world.'[137]

This event was the precursor to a regular series of lectures in this 'Theosophical library'. One day in the audience there appeared 'Marie von Sivers, who was then chosen by destiny to take on with a sure hand the leadership of the German Section of the Theosophical Society, which was founded soon after I started giving my lectures.'

This destined meeting with Marie von Sivers then led to Steiner's decision also to lead this German section spiritually. He decided to set up a periodical, *Luzifer*, to enable him to give the elementary foundations for a deepened intellectual and spiritual life. The first articles here were dedicated to the subject of 'Reincarnation and karma from the perspective of the necessary ideas of modern science'.[138] Here, and in his book *Theosophy* which was published a year later (1904), were presented in detail for the first time in the history of humanity the thoughts that lead to a concept of reincarnation, and its connection with 'karma'. Since then anyone who is prepared to pay attention to the associated phenomena, can be led in thought to the proper connections. We need not repeat this in detail here, but looking back at these writings it is clear how Rudolf Steiner—completely in accord with the first phase of the anthroposophical movement—learnt how to think these concepts livingly. Although the members had a certain reserve to begin with towards working concretely on these concepts for themselves, they nevertheless found their way into them, and year by year Steiner was able to deepen them further.

A significant step towards a broader understanding of karma came about when Steiner began writing his Mystery Dramas (1910). These were not conceived only as dramas, but as something that portrayed in dramatic form the situation of the actors and the audience. The themes that interested the members of the Theosophical Society amongst themselves and in conversations with friends, reappeared in the dialogue of the actors. The special thing here was that the members themselves performed the dramas, with each one playing the 'role' to which they were best suited. Some of them, according to tradition, did not even have to act; they were by nature identical with their part:

'Rudolf Steiner's choice of actors was masterful. In their behaviour and appearance they suited their part superbly; for the most part they could perform the role without make-up or even having to act. One simply believed the character they were embodying ...'[139] This memoir of Oskar Schmiedel's agrees with other accounts that report the same thing. Except for the main parts, Steiner gave the actors free rein in how they portrayed their role, 'and yet ... a really inexplicable effect came about,'[140] that was never achieved again in subsequent performances. 'The powerfully convincing quality of the performances of the Mystery Dramas in Munich seemed enigmatic, inexplicable to many people.'[141] When at a later time an actor asked Steiner whether this enigmatic effect was connected with the relationship the actors had with their roles, he said 'that each actor possessed a particular personal aptitude for the individuality he was representing: "They were themselves formerly once dignitaries of this kind!"'[142]

To understand a statement like this we need to bear in mind that the Mystery Dramas are not four disconnected works, but plays that not only relate to one another but also follow the characters in the dramas and their karma through a number of incarnations. They are the first dramas in which not only the re-embodiment of the human spirit is taken seriously, but also, because of this, the operation of destiny and its metamorphoses. For example, it is evident from the fourth Mystery Drama, *The Soul's Awakening,* that the present situation (in the first Drama) was set in motion in ancient Egypt.

But, as is known, the first Mystery Drama, *The Portal of Initiation,* came about as a metamorphosis of Goethe's fairy tale.[143] Even during the rehearsals in Munich in 1910, Steiner used the Goethean pictures and names, although the individual pictorial [fairy-tale] figures had already been turned into actual [human] characters. The will-o'-the-wisps had now become Capesius and Strader; the Green Snake, the Other Maria; the Spirit of the Elements had become the Ferryman, and so on. What the *Fairy Tale* was still lacking in its presentation of the being of man, and which was typical of Goethe, was the idea of reincarnation and karma. Rudolf Steiner thus completed the 'fairy-tale picture' and created an extended artistic version from this archetype.

But for the people who performed the first drama, this meant that they not only thought the idea of destiny and reincarnation, but 'performed' it. They played the particular character through different earthly lives, and could thus live into the concept of karma in a feeling way. This more feeling participation corresponds completely to the second phase of the life of the Anthroposophical Society. The idea of karma and reincarnation is now not only understood, but attains a life of its own!

Just as, at the beginning of the first phase, an individual appears through whom the further course of destiny is crystallized—namely Marie von Sivers—so the Munich impulse is also connected with a figure without whom the artistic impulse would never have got off the ground. This figure was Sophie Stinde. Not only were the performances of the Mystery Dramas due to her initiative, but also the building impulse associated with these was advanced a fair way by her. The Johannes Building, as the planned Goetheanum was first called after the main character in the first Mystery Drama, was to be built in Munich!

A further phase in the deepening of the idea of karma was reached after the end of the First World War. In the general cultural collapse, various anthroposophists decided to work out of anthroposophy in their professional life. However, this often heroic step did not always lead to the intended healing result. The degree of spiritual penetration in the specialist fields was often insufficient to renew everything, or the required self-schooling was lacking. But the collapse of many of these initiatives showed where the mistakes lay, and finally led to Steiner formulating conditions under which any responsible action out of anthroposophy could be undertaken.

Since the Christmas Conference of 1923, what was required was not only a free decision to wish to join one's own goals with anthroposophy, but also the free decision to join one's own life with the life of the Anthroposophical Society. This cannot be forced on anyone externally. But once the decision was made, it had karmic consequences! There were conditions associated with it: from now on one had to look not only after one's own progress but also that of the Anthroposophical Society. The 'sway of karma' was dissolved by a free decision for karma. This turning-point was intentionally not always easy for the comrades-in-arms; that was the nature of the thing. This even applied to Steiner himself! Without being able to see what the consequences would be for him, he too had to make a free decision to connect himself personally with the Anthroposophical Society.

Seen in this way, the Christmas Conference was not a conference in any run-of-the-mill sense, not even a conference in the anthroposophical sense of many that had preceded it. It was a 'conference' where those taking part could decide to lead their life in the future in collaboration with the Anthroposophical Society, which also meant with Rudolf Steiner. Anyone who took this risk and was prepared not only to comprehend his destiny, and not only to experience it feelingly, but also, almost as a kind of experiment, to dedicate it to something that he recognized to be necessary, got something back—and he could count on this—from the free will forces engaged in this way. Rudolf Steiner experienced this most clearly with Ita Wegman who, from Penmaenmawr onwards, had resolved to put her life entirely at the service of collaboration with Steiner, without regard for her own [personal] advancement. Steiner therefore referred to her again and again in order to show others what became possible through a total engagement of this kind. He points, for example, to how new findings in the field of medicine can be inspired if the work is taken seriously enough. Thus he speaks of Ita Wegman, 'his dear colleague', as follows:

> This research, which looks for the gateway by which to enter in the appropriate way from the physical human being into the spiritual human being, can only give promising results if it is conducted in the right way. This means that in the case of the kind of work here, not only the research forces of the present are engaged, but precisely research forces that come into the picture when one takes up the karmic threads that arise from the evolutionary history of humanity. One has to work with the forces of karma, so to speak, in order to get behind the mysteries in question.[144]

But we only become mature enough for such a way of perceiving when we connect our own karma with other people through joint work. This work is then the building-stone for a 'spiritual Goetheanum'.[145]

The transition to this third way of deepening the concept of karma came with the burning down of the first Goetheanum on New Year's Eve of 1922/23. What was destroyed by an act of arson had a deep effect on the destiny of many members. It was not only a beautiful building, a magnificent work of art, that was burnt to ashes; it was also the protective cloak of anthroposophy itself. People had already heard lectures by Steiner there, seen eurythmy performances, had themselves pondered on the forms of the building. But not only this. The loss was all the more painful because many members had participated in the building process, had taken part in the chiselling, in the painting, or had donated money. This is what made the building a work with which people had connected themselves karmically. And all this was burnt down—in one night!

The [external result of their] work could be taken away from the members, but not their common will to work on anthroposophy all the more intensively. Rudolf Steiner's response was to found the renewed Anthroposophical Society during the Christmas Conference of 1923. This gave every member the potential to practise destiny by deciding to take part. What one thought about it, what worries one had, etc., was of no interest; all that counted was whether one was ready in wishing jointly to carry

Fig. 60 Rudolf Steiner 1923.

anthroposophy further. The fact that people nevertheless got involved later with the problems they brought with them, is another story.

And here too, where the third phase of the Anthroposophical Society first begins properly to come to life, there is a figure at the outset who sought a destiny in order to bring the whole process into motion. This was Daniel Nicol Dunlop, the Scot and man of the world who, after being engaged intensively for many years in work for the Theosophical Society, met Rudolf Steiner in 1922. He then became fully involved in Steiner's work, and asked him to give a summer course on the *central theme of anthroposophy*. He offered his special 'sacred' place for this: Penmaenmawr in North Wales. He had himself already organized many summer schools in different places in England and Scotland, but his meeting with Steiner awoke in him the wish to hear something about the *central theme of anthroposophy* precisely in Penmaenmawr. This place then became a place of destiny for Rudolf Steiner. Again it is not the lectures here that gave this place its special atmosphere, nor only the human meetings that were possible there, but it was the place itself that retained a wealth of 'enduring Imaginations' from ancient times. And these were significant for Steiner, and had effects. Looking back on the trip, this also was clear to him, and he ascribed what had been gained from the event, and which 'was entered into the golden book of the anthroposophical movement,' to 'the exceptionally insightful' work of Dunlop. 'What became possible really only became so through the really spiritually insightful way that this place was chosen. I believe it is quite important to bear in mind at some point that there are such exceptional places on the earth's surface where, in such livingly enduring memory, there is directly living there what was once alive as a Sun-cult to prepare for the later acceptance of Christianity in North and West Europe.'[146] We have already seen that this is not referring to the preparation of an already-established Christianity (see page 117).

The bridge between the life of the ancient Mysteries and a new Mystery culture is initially established by an experience of karma. Every individual bears their past earthly lives and the consequences of these in themselves, even if unconsciously. Lifting these into consciousness is the task of anthroposophy. In the context of world history however, in the spiritual world from the fifteenth to the sixteenth century, the Michael School established the bridge between the ancient Mystery cultures and our time.[147] There Michael himself gave a thorough review of the ancient initiation wisdom, and looked ahead to a spiritualization of thinking. Michael's intention was to prepare the individuals who were approaching a re-birth, for their new earthly existence, so that they would be able to find anthroposophy there as the spiritual life that resonated with them. For everything

> that happens here in the physical and sensory world, happens beforehand in spiritual worlds... And precisely this is the important thing: what happens here on the earth in the twentieth century as the coming together of a number of individualities in the Anthroposophical Society, was prepared for in the first half of the nineteenth century by the souls of these people incarnated today who come together in large numbers—these were united spiritually when they had not yet descended into the physical-sensory world. And at that time in the spiritual worlds there was a kind of cultus cultivated by a number of souls who worked together—a cultus which prepared the longings that have arisen in the souls now in bodies, who come together in the Anthroposophical Society. And anyone who has the gift of recognizing these souls in their bodies, recognizes them from how they worked together with him in the first half of the nineteenth century when mighty cosmic Imaginations were placed in the supersensory worlds, which represent what I could call 'the new Christianity'.[148]

This significant cosmic cultus at the end of the eighteenth and the beginning of the nineteenth century, was the fading echo of the Michael School. What played out there in real Imaginations had a specific effect. For 'at a particularly favourable moment' a picture of this, in miniature, flowed into Goethe's mind. 'And this little miniature picture, this metamorphosed, altered little miniature picture is what is portrayed for us by Goethe in his *Fairy Tale of the Green Snake and the Beautiful Lily*. It is a situation where something softly breaks through.'[149]

Steiner refers again and again to this Michael School when speaking about the spiritual preparation for anthroposophy: 'What lives in anthroposophy was initially stimulated by the Michael School in the fifteenth, sixteenth century, and by the cultus that took place at a supersensory level at the end of the eighteenth and the beginning of the nineteenth century. It is also for this reason, and having a view to this supersensory cultus, that my Mystery Plays came into being, particularly the first Mystery which, although it has many differences from Goethe's *Fairy Tale of the Green Snake and the Beautiful Lily*, nevertheless has marked similarities. These things, which want to contain real impulses of a spiritual nature, cannot just be sucked out of one's thumb, but are definitely perceived and worked on in accord with the spiritual world.'[150] We could add that the same applies to the Christmas Conference itself. What lit up there with retrospect to the ancient Mysteries, and what was given as impulses for a spiritualization of thinking, most certainly also originated from the Michael School!

Through all ages Michael had the task of awakening an understanding of the Christ Being and of the Mystery of Golgotha. What was important for him was not so much that people merely knew certain things, but rather how they found their way independently to Christianity. Rudolf Steiner himself followed this tendency his whole life, and also observed it in Goethe. Thus he later emphasized that once Goethe had overcome his heathenism and written his *Fairy Tale*, although it does not mention Christ, nevertheless 'the way in which the images are conceived, the way the human souls are thought of in their changes ... the sequence of the thoughts, the power of the thoughts, is Christian, is the new way to Christ'.[151] Steiner wanted to link to this, and thus he disclosed the following:

'It was at the end of the eighties of the nineteenth century that... the penny dropped for me concerning this fairy tale. Since then I have never left the path that was to lead me further and further to an understanding of Goethe by means of these mighty Imaginations.' If one wished to grasp the fairy tale, it was necessary to fructify one's intellect by the ideas of spiritual science. But this meant that the intellect first had to be developed for an understanding of the Mystery of Golgotha. 'If you develop in yourself the potential to transform your soul forces such that they begin...to find the transition to the pictorial quality that Goethe strove for, you then train your soul forces in such a way that you find a new comprehension of the Mystery of Golgotha.'[152]

The decisive step on this path was taken at the Christmas Conference. The significance of this was then revealed in the great Michael lecture on 13 January 1924 and in the so-called Michael letters.

Here we will look at one aspect that can perhaps reveal why during his whole life Steiner watched Goethe's *Fairy Tale* grow, metamorphose and ripen, and returned to it again and again. We already saw that ever since his Weimar period it had enabled him to gain access to an understanding of the Michael School. But we also saw that Michael operates in the destiny of the individuals connected with him; those who seek spiritual paths while on earth were prepared for this by their participation in his School and its associated cultus.

Someone who manages to find the forces that enable him to see into the world before his birth, will encounter the Michael School a long time before birth, and the forces which shape his karma. Steiner describes it like this:

> For example, we meet with some misfortune. To begin with our feeling is that it is a misfortune. It is not easy for us to bear. But if we knew why, for decades or even centuries before our birth, we had arranged everything so that we would meet with this misfortune,

> then we would find many things a lot more bearable! ... I won't go into the general details here since you can find them in my books, but I should like to show with a few examples how life before birth influences life after birth. You see...when we have passed the midpoint of our life between death and a new birth...the inner experience of the soul in the spiritual world is then directed primarily down towards the earth. And, when we are living past this midpoint, increasingly more impressions begin to rise up to us from what is happening on the earth, what people down there are thinking and feeling, and the soul receives very particular impressions. So for example, in the second half of its spiritual life, a soul can live towards its new life, and looks down more and more at the people who, let us say, are down there preparing the subsequent age—people who are having an influence intellectually and spiritually. Certain individuals amongst these intellectually and spiritually active people become particularly valued by the soul. It even happens that from the spiritual world we look down particularly at one or two individuals who are active on earth. Someone, for example, who was born in the second half of the nineteenth century, was, we can assume, in the spiritual world at the beginning of the nineteenth and in the second half of the eighteenth century. But he gazed down at the significant individuals who influenced the culture at that time. Certain individuals amongst them are particularly valued by him, they are particularly dear to him. This is something that we experience here: that we look down to the people who are developing down there below. But by gazing down at these individuals we also have an influence on them, but not in a way that compromises their freedom. Our influence is such that certain things living in their soul rise up more easily into their soul by being gazed on by some soul or other from the spiritual world. In this way people on earth are stimulated to work, to activity, by souls who will be born later than these people on earth, and who gaze down on them.[153]

It is not hard to connect the processes described here by Steiner with his own life before birth. And the soul on which he gazed, who was among the leading individuals in the life of thought, was Goethe. From the spiritual world, he helped Goethe to receive the inspiration of *The Fairy Tale*. Where Steiner writes about this in *The Course of My Life*, as we have already seen, he describes how Goethe himself had the impression that inspiration had been involved in this story. This is also why Goethe did not occupy himself further with its content. Although he collected other people's interpretations of it, no interpretation of his own could be enticed out of him for the rest of his life. It shone down into his life from a higher realm without being able to awaken in him a higher striving. For Steiner, however, the fairy tale was *the* wake-up call from the Michael School. Once he had recognized it, he never let it go; he took it into his mediations, metamorphosed it into his first Mystery Drama, smelted it down and recast it a second time in order finally, after the Christmas Conference, to reveal its origin.

If we bear all this in mind, we are granted, from the lecture just quoted above, a look into the workshop of Rudolf Steiner's destiny, by which many things become more understandable. For Steiner continues the description as follows:

> It has happened, for example, that someone living as a soul in the spiritual world during the eighteenth and the first half of the nineteenth century, took one of the exceptional individuals of the earthly world as his ideal; he then wanted to be like this individual, wanted to strive in the same way as he after his birth. For example, one sees the books by someone whom one wishes to emulate after one's birth. One thus looks down from heaven to the earth with a certain inner longing, with a certain inner urge in the way that—albeit with a somewhat different feeling—one looks as a living person with longing to the 'beyond', to heaven. The considerable difference, however, is that when as an earthly individual one looks up to heaven without knowledge of spiritual science, it remains fairly indistinct. But a characteristic of the human being in heaven, living in the spiritual world, is that he sees with particular clarity from the spiritual world the situation on earth, the human soul that he particularly venerates, whose writings he will perhaps read.

When Rudolf Steiner comes to the earth he finds here the results of the destiny he took part in determining. He takes it up with enthusiasm and interest, and thus it can expand in ever-growing circles [of people] as a blessing for his fellow human beings. That precisely in the twentieth century karma has such a force that it is initially received as an idea but then develops into something leading to free decisions, is connected with the fact that precisely today the time has begun when Christ has become the Lord of karma of this kind[154] in order to shape and structure the consequences of human deeds for the good of humankind. In Rudolf Steiner's earthly life this impulse comes into effect in a way that can be observed for the first time.

The Founding of the New Mysteries

In the previous pages we followed how the Anthroposophical Society came into being—a society that concerns itself with how the spirit is at work in nature and the human being; a society that follows the paths of the deceased and lays importance on knowing why the human spirit repeatedly decides to enter a new earthly existence, and how its destiny is shaped thereby and comes to expression; a society that is interested in all this not just theoretically but also engages practically, initially in modern art, creating a new 'organic' architecture, but then also in the broader cultural life of our times seeking to transform it towards a more spiritual goal worthy of the human being. A society of this nature, whose actions are so contrary to the comfortable trends of our time, cannot have arisen simply out of the normal flow of contemporary culture. Even if we take into account the tremendous energy in Steiner's work, and feel that what he stimulated came from him personally, the reality of such a cultural impulse nevertheless still remains incomprehensible. It is clear from what we have seen so far that for Rudolf Steiner himself his experience of past mysteries, mysteries apparently long gone, inspired him to many aspects of renewal. But where does the energy for such an impulse come from, and where do the members and colleagues draw [their impetus] from?

In earlier ages of human development the answer would have been easy to find. It would have been the gods, or at least spiritual beings, who inspired people and led them. Influences of this kind still occurred in Abraham's time and were accepted without doubt. But these influences went into abeyance and grew weaker. The gods withdrew to the same extent that humanity became more earthly. Finally it was the prophets alone who were still open to the divine voice, and as prophets too became increasingly rare, only dreams remained as the means by which revelations from the gods [could be received]. In his *Apology*, Socrates still invokes Apollo who came to him in dreams and urged him to his task of training people's thinking.

It was also the gods who founded the mysteries in order to help humanity in its cultural development, indeed even to make this possible in the first place. And they founded them in accordance with the inherent potential of a specific time and place. Hence the fundamental differences, for example, between the mysteries of the northern and the southern peoples. The northern peoples sought to elucidate the cosmos with everything this involves, from nature in a narrow sense right up to the heavenly bodies and the inhabitants of the stars. The southern peoples had the task of researching the human being, with the different members of his being [his subtle bodies etc.], his repeated incarnations, and his metamorphoses. As a result of their different powers of vision, an initiate of the Egyptian mysteries eventually knew everything concerning the human being, and structured his culture accordingly, whereas the initiate of the northern mysteries ultimately had an understanding of the whole cosmos, and organized from this the structuring of the northern cultural stream. Only in Greek culture does an impulse first emerge for structuring a middle way where man and world are seen as belonging together. This was the mystery stream that was then in a position to prepare an understanding of the Christ Being who, as the Creator Being of the world, became man and dwelt among us (see the Prologue of St John's Gospel).

Through the Mystery of Golgotha the entire human situation was changed. Whereas previously, when they sought genuine initiation experience, people had tended away from the earth towards the sun, from now onwards it was the earth that was the spiritual focal-point of existence. For when the One who had previously been the Sun God descended to us and proclaimed he would remain henceforth with human beings on the earth, then the whole institution of the ancient mysteries, which was connected to a transported [i.e. out-of-body] experience of the Sun God, had to disappear.

And it did indeed happen that the mysteries faded away and lost their power. They closed of their own accord. There were still some 'last' oracular statements from a number of famous sites indicating that after these the gods no longer wanted to speak to human beings there. This was not only connected externally to the spread of Christianity, but also internally as a result of the Mystery of Golgotha. People had to learn to lead their lives independently, free from any divine influence, and to build on their own foundation.

This developmental step also applied to Rudolf Steiner who never gave up on it. Although he did indeed seek to link up with the ancient mysteries, what he sought there was not to re-establish the old consciousness prevalent at that time—this had been overcome and remained so—but he sought to link up with the ancient treasuries of wisdom that were once protected and cultivated in those places. What interested Steiner was what the initiates of those times had researched with their ancient methods and the spiritual findings they had attained, and he attempted to find these again in the akasha chronicle. His method consisted in extracting and reading what we as human beings wrote in past earth lives in the 'memory of evolution'.

He describes this process which has to be applied today, in the great Michael lecture of 13 January 1924[155], as follows:

> You see, just as our memory, our internal memory for the ordinary things we experience in earthly life, retains things for us, so it is the astral light [that does the same] with what we have written into it, and spreads out around us representing a written tablet of the secrets we ourselves have inscribed into it. This is also what we have to read if we wish to reach the mysteries once more. It is a kind of memory of evolution that needs to arise in humanity. And an awareness that such a memory of evolution exists must gradually emerge; humanity must read the astral light with regard to its previous cultural epochs in the same way as we, when we are older, read our youth through our ordinary memory. Because this needs to come to people's consciousness, I have here given during the Christmas period precisely the lectures that I have given in such a way that shows you that it is truly a matter of drawing the secrets we need today out of the astral light.

In this way Steiner can then make a connection with the Greek 'mysteries of light' when he seeks to spiritualize thinking; he can make a connection with the Egyptian 'mysteries of space' when he has to renew the artistic impulse; and he can make a connection with the megalithic 'mysteries of the earth'[156] to transform civilization in general. The threefold nature of the ancient mysteries thus becomes the inspirer of a new threefold culture. Ultimately the idea of a 'threefold social organism' grew entirely out of the impulses to renew the three kinds of ancient mysteries. Anyone looking at this connection will understand how to evaluate Steiner's initial efforts to form a society in which some kind of interest could develop for the ancient mysteries, because it experienced how fruitful such an interest can be. That his ideas for cultural renewal arose out of a real experience of the flow of time, is something one could experience again and again. We could say that what was done by Rudolf Steiner did indeed transfer ancient mystery secrets over into our culture, so that we could make a connection with them and take them further, but this was not a renewal of the mysteries themselves! That required more—more practical application and far more understanding. For what are the mysteries actually, and why is it so difficult to form a proper idea of them?

When we approach them externally, the mysteries are first of all schools where individuals, having been chosen by spiritual beings, are educated and trained by initiate teachers and prepared for initiation. We must picture this education and preparation for initiation as a strict training whose various levels involved trials that required all the novice's strength to overcome. In ancient times they were not just schools where one learnt things but places of schooling that changed and transformed the individual's whole soul life.

> The preparation the would-be initiate had to undergo in those times is something the modern person is not keen to form an idea about... because this idea irritates him. The individual of today would like to undergo initiation wherever possible like something incidental one takes along on one's path through life, something one achieves as a side-issue. He would like to inform himself—as one calls it nowadays—about what leads to [spiritual] knowledge, but this modern person would not like to experience what the people in ancient times who sought initiation had to experience. To be taken hold of in his entire being by the preparation for knowledge, to become a different person—this is not something he is keen to do. But those people [in ancient times] had to resolve to become another person. ...The essential preparation of the individual in ancient times was that he had to undergo the inner condition of soul that can be designated with one word by saying: he had to be led, in the strongest possible way, through the *fear* which a human being always feels when, in full consciousness, he is really and truly brought before something completely unknown to him. This was precisely the essential aspect in the old initiations, that the people had to really absorb the feeling that they were confronted with something they could not meet in any way in outer life ... The soul constitution with which people...in those ancient times wanted to gain knowledge was essentially different. It could have nothing in common with the soul forces that served outer life; they had to stem, so to speak, from completely different regions of the human being. These regions are always there in the human being, but people have a terrible fear of having to deal with them ... Therefore we can describe it externally—but it should be understood more inwardly—as the bringing about of a series of states of fear, which nevertheless had to be undergone because only that which lives in the human soul in a region which in ordinary outer life people are afraid of, can be led to intentional knowledge.[157]

Overcoming these states of fear is bound up with a purification of the soul life. If this did not happen sufficiently, and if one were unaware that [these states of fear] must always arise when crossing the threshold, one would shrink back from the immeasurable terror that is connected with experiencing the Guardian, and not be able to enter the spiritual world.

If an individual was sufficiently advanced in their preparation however, then the actual initiation could be gazed on which took place in a death-sleep over three and a half days:

> This was the ancient method of attaining initiation—first bringing the soul to a state of sufficient maturity, doing everything by way of preparation to make the soul mature; then being put into a state for three and a half days in which one was completely [absent and] remote from the external world, and also from the instruments with which we perceive the external world. This is why those who were to be led into the spiritual world were carefully prepared beforehand; their soul was prepared to cognize spiritual life. Then they were withdrawn from the world for three and a half days, and taken to a place for this purpose where they could not perceive anything with their outer senses, where their body was in a death-like condition. And after three days they were awoken once more; their soul was called back into their body. Individuals of this nature were then able to remember what they had seen in the higher worlds, and to bear witness to the spiritual worlds themselves. This was the great secret of initiation, that the soul, after long preparation, was led out of the body into a completely different world for three and a half days; it was closed to the outer world and penetrated into the spiritual world.[158]

Even this level in the initiate's life could be transcended, so that the initiate could advance further by stages. He gave up his private life in order to serve the community. Within the community he mediated the intentions of the gods with what was possible on earth, in a way in keeping with a healthy civilization. An initiate cannot be imagined without his community; and the community in turn was dependent in its cultural life on the initiate. Initiates were practical people; their faculties and tasks involved reaching right into the technical and scientific aspects of life.

From the third century B.C. there had been three different kinds of mysteries with three different schooling paths which had revealed true [spiritual] knowledge in three different areas of the earth. Because of this there were also three kinds of culture. Each culture had specific areas which it cultivated in a particular one-sided way—thus the intellectual life in Greece, the life of rights in ancient Egypt, and the economic life in megalithic culture.[159]

Around the time of Christ's birth the ancient mystery practices began to lose their energy, but the cultures connected with them lived on for a long time from their effects. Even blossoming Christianity lived on in

Rome and Constantinople in the stream of antique culture, whereas in northern Europe the megalithic-Celtic stream continued to work right into the Middle Ages. Only then do these streams slowly lose their one-sidedness and begin unconsciously and gradually to weave together.

After the knowledge of the pre-Christian mysteries had been almost completely extinguished for centuries, in Goethe's time the first serious memories of it re-emerge. Surprisingly, the masonic lodges that were expanding at that time, knew of their Egyptian origins and were proud of them.[160] On the other hand, classical scholars discover the Greek mystery institutions but without inwardly perceiving what they were. [They see them as] a phenomenon among other religious phenomena which interested people particularly in the later period of Greek culture. To begin with the northern or Celtic mysteries still remain completely unknown. All this is changed by Schelling. The stories and myths of various peoples had interested him already in his youth, and by reflecting on 'Nature' and its spiritual qualities he soon began to take the Greek mystery traditions seriously. His first presentation of this was in a small book whose title reveals his intention: *Bruno, oder über das göttliche und natürliche Princip der Dinge* (Bruno, or on the divine and natural principle of things).[161] It takes the form of a dialogue in Platonic style on what meaning the mysteries really had for Greece: 'The purpose of the mysteries was none other than to show people the archetypes of everything which they otherwise usually only have in reflected form.' There 'people learnt for the first time that apart from the things that are constantly undergoing change and multiformal transformation, there is something unchanging, of one form, and indivisible.' In addition to this, the mysteries were seen as a place where those 'who participated in them were brought, through a purification of soul, to a re-remembering of previously perceived Ideas of the True, the Beautiful, and the Good, and thereby to the highest blessedness. Since exulted philosophy consists in knowledge of the Eternal and the Unchanging, the teachings of the mysteries were thus none other than the most sublime, the most sacred and most excellent philosophy passed on as tradition from external antiquity, so that the mysteries really relate to mythology in the same way, so we believe, as philosophy relates to poetry...'[162]

Schelling anticipated finding the sublime philosophy of the True, the Beautiful, and the Good in the Greek mysteries of Eleusis. When he later conceived his idea of *Weltalter* (Ages of the World)—a work he laboured on his whole life but could only produce in fragmentary form—he had in mind an overview of world evolution in its entirety, from its existence in the past and via development in the present to the goal of the future. *Past,*

Present, and Future was also the subtitle of the first version in 1811, whose first lines were to read: 'The past is known, the present is perceived, the future is sensed in presentiment.' Here for the first time the fundamental idea lit up for him upon which all his further philosophizing was based; all the magnificent work he continued to elaborate, from his *Philosophy of Mythology* to his *Philosphy of Revelation,* was overshone by this idea. But in order to understand our spiritual origins we need the mysteries, and since in Schelling's day no work had as yet been done in this area, Schelling set about working on it himself. In 1815 he published a small work, *Über die Gottheiten von Samothrake* (On the divinities of Samothrace), with the subtitle: *A Supplement to the Ages of the World*. What Schelling accomplished with this is almost impossible to estimate today. For here his zeal for research entered new territory. As much as his extensive knowledge of languages allowed, he combed through all the literature of antiquity for references to Samothrace in order to bring to light what had once been living there spiritually. Of the 131 references known today, Schelling already knew 127 of them—an achievement that was concealed in his extensive notes. His surprising result concerning the core of the Samothracian mysteries was his discovery that 'Michael' had been active there, whose name in Samothrace was Kadmilos [or Cadmilus]. But *Kadmos* [or Cadmus] indicates a connection with the Phoenicians for whom he is the messenger of the gods (and brother of Europa), who as 'the Glow of Dawn' proclaims the sunrise. With this 'morning call' Schelling then sets about his further research into the Greek mystery institutions, and in 1828 is finally far enough to venture a presentation of the mysteries of Eleusis in his lectures.[163] He was never able to complete his *Ages of the World* because he simply lacked the knowledge concerning the ancient mystery sites. But the basic idea continued to mature to the point of the glorious perspectives that he felt able to commit to manuscript in his later years in Berlin. The divine existence of the Father-God of the past is led further, via the activity of the divine Son-God in the knowledge of the present, to a perception of the future in the Spirit.

His contemporaries had nothing but scorn and derision for this great design which Schelling presented publicly only once in his first semester in Berlin; he could therefore find no other option but to keep his pearls to himself. He made improvements to his manuscript here and there, but without giving attention to the unity of the work.

These works only began to speak once more for Rudolf Steiner, specifically during the same period when he was working with Goethe's works in Weimar. While his acquaintance with Goethe led him to a mystical experience of the Mystery of Golgotha, something similar happened with his work on Schelling. Steiner only spoke of this right at the end in one of his final lectures. In this lecture[164] Steiner turns again to his great discovery of the Michael School, founded in spiritual worlds from the fourteenth to the eighteenth century, with the aim of addressing the human beings who were not incarnated at that time, and giving to those who had the preparation for it the impulse to take these truths and, when on the Earth once more, to develop them into active forces within civilization. 'Michael himself [was active] as the teacher, looking back at everything that encompassed the great teachings of the ancient mysteries, giving a wonderful overview of the secrets of these ancient mysteries, but at the same time giving a mighty preview of what was to come.'[165] This Michael School came to a close with a 'significant, supersensory cultus' at the end of the eighteenth and beginning of the nineteenth century, which, in real Imaginations, presented the whole context once more in living pictures.

Goethe drew from these pictures to compose his fairy tale, and Steiner drew from them to compose his first Mystery Drama, as we discussed earlier. But that was not all: in the final analysis the whole of anthroposophy can be traced back to this Michael School:

> But you see, my dear friends, if we take anthroposophy with its present content and trace it backwards, we find little preparation for it on earth. If you go back a bit from what has emerged as anthroposophy today, and look with an open mind...to find sources somewhere for this anthroposophy in the course of the nineteenth century—you won't find any. You find individual traces of a spiritual view which could be used like seeds, but very sparse seeds, for the whole framework of anthroposophy; but a proper preparation for it within the earthly realm is just not there. But all the stronger is the preparation in the supersensory sphere. And in the final analysis the extent to which Goethe's activity, including after his death,... has played into the shaping of anthroposophy, is something you are all well aware of.[166]

Something similar also applies to the other German idealists who seem to Rudolf Steiner to have a 'very strong spiritual tinge'. 'But one has to go still deeper; then one finds curious things appearing in the intellectual life of the first half of the nineteenth century... The philosopher Schelling is particularly interesting, and becomes more interesting the more one reads and is absorbed by him.' After a brief description of Schelling's early life, in which he makes a connection to Fichte, reference is made to the speedy expansion of his thinking, 'and we see ideas entering him, albeit fashioned imaginatively, but nevertheless ideas that are tending almost towards Imaginations... Then we see how Platonism almost revives in Schelling. He writes a dialogue, *Bruno*, concerning the nature of the world, that really reminds us of Plato's dialogues, and is very impressive... Then Schelling is silent for an awfully long time. He was considered by his fellow philosophers to be one of the living dead, if I can put it like that, and subsequently only published his extraordinarily significant book on *The Samothracian Mysteries*.' And Steiner also experienced in Schelling's *Philosophy of Mythology* and his *Philosophy of Revelation* a re-awakening of the ancient philosophy concerning the gods. 'In his *Philosophy of Revelation* there is, in what he says about Christianity, a significant impetus, albeit in very abstract form, for what has to be said also within anthroposophy from spiritual perception concerning many things to do with Christianity.'

Steiner worked on these subjects again and again, particularly during his time in Weimar. 'Schelling, who since 1854 had been in the spiritual world once more, came exceptionally close to one precisely through this dialogue *Bruno*, when one studied it and lived it, through his work *Clara*, and particularly through his book on *The Samothracian Mysteries*. One easily came into the real, genuine, spiritual proximity of Schelling.'

When he sought to find the spiritual foundations of the Michael age, it was to this [individual] in the realm of the dead, and to his steadily growing understanding of the evolution of the world, that Rudolf Steiner turned. 'Then, in order to get behind certain things, in 1897 I took up Schelling's *Gottheiten von Samothrake* (The divinities of Samothrace) and his *Philosophie der Mythologie* (Philosophy of Mythology) once more, really just as a stimulus. ... But actually I had in mind what had taken place in the course of the nineteenth century in such a way that it could then flow down, as it were, and become anthroposophy.' Through these inspired books he then found the path to the being of Michael himself.[167] He found the Michael cultus, the Michael School, and the whole connection of Michael with the life of the pre-Christian mysteries. He saw the twofold nature of all the mysteries, which began with a preparatory stage—the so-called 'lesser mysteries'—in which the individual was trained intellectually so that, being nourished on truths, he learnt to purify his soul life from forming mere opinions, before being allowed any access to the 'greater mysteries'. This fundamental law in the life of all the mysteries applied in all ages: the first stage was study, the learning and digesting of spiritual-scientific concepts, and only then came vision and one's own [spiritual] experience. The opposite path always leads to illusion and an exaggerated opinion of oneself, and never to anything of practical use!

This law still applies today even if the effort required for it is often underestimated. Rudolf Steiner certainly followed it from the start, and repeatedly emphasized its importance. A person who wanted to attain vision without study, without training their thinking, would first of all be plagued by terrible visions that they wouldn't know how to deal with, and would become psychologically ill, and secondly they would not be able to gain knowledge of anything of a true nature because they would of necessity misinterpret what they see. For one seeking for truth in Plato's Academy, the first fundamental condition was a rigorous training in thinking. And this took fifty years![168] This preparatory school for a schooling in the mysteries, which had arisen from the mysteries of Eleusis, lived on for centuries in order to lay the foundation for a true understanding of Christ.

As mentioned above, the turning-point in the life of the mysteries was the Mystery of Golgotha itself. Christ came to humankind, passed through death, and sent the Holy Spirit. Because of this, any kind of access to the spiritual world was now different. The fundamental law of all the mysteries still holds true: no enlightenment without catharsis. But actual 'vision' is now possible on earth and not only in the hereafter beyond death. The resurrection had an effect for all people (1 Cor. 15), and if they wanted to school themselves—something they had now to decide on freely for themselves—the spiritual world could come to meet them in blessing. Being chosen from above no longer takes place.

This change in the practice of initiation is connected with the fact that since the Mystery of Golgotha what could only be experienced beyond death has entered into life here on earth:

> That which gives us, as modern human beings in our present life on earth, the freedom and the capacity to think in abstractions, is what comes in the opposite direction from the one we ourselves take when we pass through the portal of death, and comes from heavenly worlds into the earthly world. We pass through the portal of death and out into spiritual worlds. Our freedom and capacity for abstraction is a heavenly gift that has come into the earthly world from supersensory worlds. This permeates us with a feeling for what we are as human beings by being able to pervade us inwardly with the consciousness not only that we bear a spiritual element within us, but where we have this spiritual element from. We turn our gaze towards death and say: What lies beyond death is something that a more ancient humanity learnt to know in a very particular way. It has now entered [the earth], and the person of today learns to know

> it between birth and death. And because this heavenly element—intellectuality and freedom—has entered earthly life, it has become necessary to look up to divinity in a different way than was the case in earlier times. And this different way of looking up to divinity has become possible for humanity through the Mystery of Golgotha. By the Christ entering into earthly life, he can sanctify what has come from supersensory worlds and which otherwise would lead humanity astray into arrogance and all sorts of other things. We live in a time when we have to understand that the most sacred thing we have in this age—the capacity to conceive pure concepts and the capacity for freedom—must be permeated by the Christ impulse ... People need to learn pure thinking with Christ, to be a free being with Christ, because otherwise that which has come over for them into the sensory from the supersensory world will not be perceived by them in the right way in its connection with the supersensory world. Here we stand, and when we look at ourselves as modern human beings we know that the supersensory element has entered earthly life through the portal of death but in the opposite direction from the one that we take when we pass through the portal of death. This is what happens in us human beings. What happens in the world is that Christ, the Spirit-Sun, has descended into earthly worlds so that what has entered at a human level into the sensory from the supersensory can find what has descended at a cosmic level into the sensory from the supersensory, so that the human being and the Spirit of the Cosmos can find each other and come together in the right way. For the human being can only stand properly in the world when the spirit within him finds the spirit outside him in the right way. The spirit, which for ancient humanity lived on the other side of death, can only be properly possessed by modern humanity during life on earth, when at the same time the human being is shone upon and illumined by that which descended to earth as Christ from the worlds out of which rationality, intellectuality, and freedom have descended into human life between birth and death.[169]

So, what the former initiate could see only after death and out of the body, must be found in human life today in full consciousness while within the body. And this has consequences with respect to all striving for knowledge. In the first place, the starting point is always in our logical thinking. From there, through training, it can be expanded in multiple ways but will never reach the point of being able to survey the entire network of ideas which is capable of infinite growth. Also one's mental power is generally never as great as it would need to be to have everything one has already worked on at one's fingertips. For as long as we are alive, the body presents an obstacle to comprehensive knowledge, even with intense training in thinking. But there is a possibility which nevertheless gives hope for a growing knowledge. And Rudolf Steiner shows us this in the example of Christ-understanding itself.

Our 'normal' intellect is not able to comprehend the Mystery of Golgotha. This was also the case during the lifetime of the apostles who, though aware that something significant was happening, did not understand what it really was. They had only an inkling, due to the vestige of atavistic clairvoyance they still possessed, of who it was that walked among them.

> But the human soul continues to develop even after it has passed through the portal of death. This human soul that continues to develop after passing through the portal of death also continues to grow after death with respect to its forces of understanding; it learns to understand more and more. Now the curious thing is that the contemporaries of Christ who, through their love of Christ, had prepared themselves for life in Christ after death, only comprehended the Mystery of Golgotha fully out of their own human forces in the third century after the Mystery of Golgotha. So those who had lived at the same time as Christ as his disciples and apostles subsequently died and lived on in the spiritual world; and while they were living in the spiritual world their forces also grew in the same way as they do here [on earth]. Now, when we die our understanding is not so advanced as it is two centuries after we have died. It was actually not until the second or towards the third century that the contemporaries [of Christ] had advanced sufficiently there in the spiritual realm where the human being abides between death and a new birth, that they came to an understanding out of themselves of what they had experienced here on the earth two to three centuries before. And from the spiritual world they then inspired people who were down here on earth. From this perspective read what the so-called church fathers wrote in the second or third century when this inspiration really began.[170]

In the same way that a living contact came about between 'dead' Goethe and living Rudolf Steiner, through which Goethe was able to inspire Steiner, a contact arose at that time between the individual apostles and the church fathers, through which the church fathers came to the inspirations they were seeking. One of these early fathers was Origen (185-254 CE).

He did not only 'understand' what the dead could now tell him because their understanding of the Mystery of Golgotha had grown, he also grasped whom it was he should thank for these inspirations and why they were possible at all. To be capable of receiving inspirations, one needed to have worked spiritually and strengthened one's thinking. A person who did this, however, had the most glorious perspective after his death:

> One who with great diligence cultivates pious religious study in this life may acquire only a small part of the great, immeasurable treasury of divine knowledge; but he already gains great benefit by directing his mind towards a loving effort to research the truth, thereby making himself ready to receive a future education. It is like someone who wishes to paint a portrait and first of all makes a shadowy outline with fine pencil of the later form, and prepares a sketch which can then have the face painted over it ...It follows from this that those who already have a sketchy indication of the truth and of knowledge in this life, will be given in the future life the beauty of the completed picture ...
>
> After we have conceived a zeal and desire on earth for knowledge of this nature, the [full] knowledge and insight of it will be given to us after death ...I believe that, once they have departed this life, all the saints abide in a place on the earth which in holy scripture is called 'Paradise', which is like a place of learning, the lecture hall as it were, of a school for souls. There they are given instruction concerning everything they have seen on earth, and also receive indications of what is to come in the future...[171]

What Origen describes here is not only documenting our after-death growth in knowledge for which we prepare sketchily in life, but this deepened interest in spiritual questions allows those participating in them to become members of the School of Michael. The Michael School does not consist simply of a regular elaboration of the knowledge we gained on earth, but has the task of *preparing* people for their future life in the age of Michael, so that when they are born in our age they can remember the higher goals!

Intellectual preparation as the prerequisite for any kind of spiritual life is as applicable today as it ever was: on the one hand, in content, so that we really 'know' something about the spiritual world; but also, on the other hand, in methodology, so that we learn how to grasp supersensory forms when they wish to be inspired. In Goethe's time people were satisfied with developing their powers of thought and were grateful to have achieved any step forward. An indication of this was the general interest in the broadening of consciousness, along with the joy people had in their own intellectual development. And not least, artistic expression showed the self-determined tasks individuals had set for themselves. This was something that Goethe and the whole circle of individuals connected with him gladly devoted themselves to. But they were not yet ready to intervene in the culture [of their day] at a practical level.

This changed only in the twentieth century. From the moment Rudolf Steiner was prepared to take on the spiritual guidance of a circle of people associated with him, he had before him the shining higher goal of shaping cultural life once more, as in the ancient mysteries. The prerequisite for this to succeed, however, is continuous schooling!

Therefore, during the re-founding of the Anthroposophical Society at the Christmas conference of 1923, the great importance was stressed for the members who wanted to act out of anthroposophy in any area of life—whether as doctor, teacher, or businessman—that they practise a genuine meditative life. Anyone unwilling to take on this obligation cannot operate in the name of anthroposophy. For anyone who gives their work an anthroposophical direction, is at the same time a representative of anthroposophy whether they wish to be or not. Of course, someone who becomes a member of the Anthroposophical Society just in order to get to know anthroposophy, does naturally not need to undertake such an obligation. But if one wishes to work outwardly out of anthroposophy, one must also want to work in harmony with others who act likewise.

One does not become a representative by being chosen, nor through the rule of destiny. One becomes a representative through a free decision. It is a decision to work with others! [We say to ourselves:] No matter what direction I have come from, my sights are not set there but on the direction I wish to go in.

The outcome of the Christmas Conference that should be striven for by the gathered members is the wish to work and act out of spiritual impulses. Rudolf Steiner calls this the idea of 'the spiritual Goetheanum'. 'We have laid the foundation stone here [meaning the Foundation Stone verse]. The building is to be erected on this Foundation Stone, whose individual stones will be the work done now in all our groups by individuals out in the wide world. Let us focus on this work.'[172]

For this to happen, Steiner established a High School at the Christmas Conference, which was organized into subject departments, into 'sections'. People can meet there who, according to their ability and education, wish to renew their specialist field through anthroposophy. This does not happen as a renewal of the one-sidedness of the ancient mystery institutions. Medicine, for example, is not developed from a transformation of the Egyptian mysteries, nor from a transformation of the Greek mysteries, nor from a transformation of the northern mystery stream, but from a harmonizing of all three forms of one-sidedness into a new unity. A renewed spiritual life will have to take the form shown in the Foundation Stone verse, from which not a single stanza could be omitted. This will then be evident right into diagnosis technology, into methods of treatment, and into medicines, which never feel obliged to take a one-sided therapeutic approach. It concerns an expansion of medicine, but an expansion that is conscious of its broader unity.

Agriculture too will no longer be renewed in its old one-sidedness but, from its living connection with the world, will be oriented towards the human being for whom it should produce healthy food. Thus Steiner had originally wanted to have agriculture and medicine together in *one* section of the High School.

Wherever we look, in whichever section, [we find] *the old streams have ceased* in favour of a new collaboration. Since all the ancient streams were one-sided, they could never bring about a destiny that gave up the one-sidednesses in favour of a unified threefoldness. What Steiner wanted to establish in the High School of Spiritual Science had to be kept clear of the 'reigning destiny', otherwise it would not be able to fulfil its task. The task, however, consisted in being a *preparatory school* for a future renewal of the mysteries, a renewal that took the schooling potential of our present times into account. This task was stated again and again after the Christmas Conference:

> The time has now come when the mysteries must be found again. They must be found again. We must be fully aware that institutions have to be set up in the present time to find the mysteries once again. The Christmas Conference was held on the basis of this awareness, for it is an urgent necessity that there be a place on the earth where the mysteries can be founded once more. In its further progress, the Anthroposophical Society must become the *way* to the renewed mysteries. This, my dear friends, will also be its task: to actively participate in this on the basis of the proper consciousness.[173]

The process necessary to enable this task to be taken up by a sufficient number of people, is threefold:

Firstly, each member who wishes to collaborate in the task must be clear as to why the mysteries need to be reinstituted today. But this can only be discovered when sufficient progress has been made on the path of deepened thinking, which is really the only thing that can give one a sense of how spirituality is lacking in our culture. Otherwise one would be satisfied with the situation as we find it. This is an indication regarding method rather than content. For it can very well happen that someone could speak about angels without having the faintest idea that in order to understand [them] a higher consciousness is necessary. Bringing about this spiritualization of consciousness is the reason for the first class of the High School of Spiritual Science.

Secondly, those members who have schooled themselves sufficiently and purified their soul life to a certain degree, should come together to work jointly, as a higher scientific community, on specific tasks. This could also happen for artistic projects; but even in the purely 'scientific' tasks, we need an artistic frame of mind if we wish to reach common results. In order to maintain a constant consciousness for these tasks, a second class was to have been introduced into the High School of Spiritual Science.

Thirdly, the members who had received ideas in the second class to stimulate a transformation of our civilization, and who had also developed the ability to put these into practice, should then have actually influenced our culture. Their experience there could then have flowed back into the High School. This was supposed to happen in a third class of the High School of Spiritual Science.

Now we could of course say that all this is already happening today. Projects do exist with groups of dedicated people, and there are institutions which do indeed have an influence on our cultural development. But from the standpoint presented in this book, this all still corresponds to the first class. Of course many beneficial things can flow from this. But what was intended only becomes evident when we are really clear as to what the mysteries truly are!

The plan for a high school of spiritual science was to have opened the way to a new life of the mysteries. 'As an age approaches that is once again more spiritual, people will indeed develop what today, in their dullness [of consciousness], they have not yet developed. But it will be necessary above all that the knowledge, the vision, the experience of the spiritual which can be drawn from present-day initiation, should be met with high estimation, reverence, out of freedom. For without being valued, without reverence, a true knowledge, a spiritual life for humanity, is actually not possible.'[174] That Steiner is including the anthroposophists here becomes clear when we follow the foundation that is intended to show what he actually meant. He says here:

> For it is so that people come back again and again into earthly existence in repeated earth lives. They thereby carry what they experienced in previous epochs over into later epochs. Human beings are

> the most important link in relation to the further development of what happens in human history. But of course people live at all times in particular surroundings. And one of the most important surroundings are the surroundings of the mysteries. One of the most important factors in human progress is the carrying over of what people have experienced in the mysteries, and then experiencing it again, whether in the mysteries once more where their influence flows out into humanity, or whether in some way in understanding. Today it has to be in understanding in some way, for the actual life of the mysteries has more or less withdrawn from the external world of today, and must first re-emerge. We have to say: The true situation is that when, through the Christmas Conference, the impulse has really gone out from here, from the Goetheanum, and has really established itself in the Anthroposophical Society by leading to the classes that are still to be established ... [it] will be the foundation for the further life of the mysteries. The further life of the mysteries must be consciously planted through the Anthroposophical Society.[175]

But here it is a matter of anthroposophy, 'in some way in understanding,' being in a position to retrieve the deeply buried but still extant previous experiences of the mysteries. If this were achieved, we would be a step further in planting the new mysteries. Today, for objective reasons, it is no longer a matter of drawing spiritual content from the inner recesses of the human soul as the ancient initiates did. That would make everything muddy. The important thing today is to learn to read once more what we inscribed in ancient times into the astral light. 'It is really a matter of retrieving from the astral light the mysteries that we need today.'[176] If we manage this, and if we then 'carry up in thoughts' what we have found, we do indeed meet Michael, if we have developed the capacities for this ... But Michael is a singular being. Michael is a being who reveals nothing unless one brings something towards him from the earth that is the result of diligent spiritual work. Michael is a silent spirit ... For what we experience of Michael is actually not his word but...his gaze, the power of his look. And this is because Michael is most concerned with the spiritual work that human beings do. He lives in the consequences of human activity.

This is also the reason why today we must find our way in freedom to the [spiritual] content we need. Michael will not reveal anything more if we do not prepare ourselves to carry up in the form of thoughts what we have experienced, and then to wait and see what results from them. Rudolf Steiner never tired of explaining that, if anything is to be achieved, we need to study: 'Therefore the right thing for souls of the present time is to retrieve into consciousness the forgotten impressions of ancient times. And how does this retrieval happen? In the way we do it in anthroposophy! Nothing new is brought before our souls, but what is retrieved is what souls experienced in earlier times.'[177]

What applies to knowledge applies equally to a new life of the mysteries. What needs to happen can only come about as the spiritual consequence by which Michael answers the retrieved ancient mystery experiences! Thus, as a preparation for the Christmas Conference, Steiner gave the lecture cycle *Myteriengestaltungen* (The Mysteries and their different forms); during the conference he gave the cycle *World History in the Light of Anthroposophy;* and after the conference, the cycle on *Mysterienstätten des Mittelalters* (Mystery centres in the Middle Ages), in order to set strings vibrating in our souls which had not formerly sounded. It was like in the Michael School in which 'the ancient initiation wisdom was thoroughly surveyed,'[178] how it had been cultivated in the various mystery centres.

The more intensively we immerse ourselves in the historical evolutionary process, the more we learn to live in the stream of time and to discern the forces upon which history depends—including the history of our age. Spiritual study, undertaken in the proper way, 'somehow in understanding', first needs to concern itself with the treasures of wisdom from the ancient mysteries, since without this knowledge we can carry nothing up to Michael in our thoughts. That there is a vast treasury to be discovered here regarding method, becomes clear when we read what George William Russell says concerning reading in the memory of the Earth. It opened up for him, and he learnt to research in sacred places, in ancient sites, what once took place there externally and spiritually. What moved him most, however, were the images of ancient mystery events:

> For those to whom in their spiritual evolution these apparitions arise I would say: try to become the master of your vision, and seek for and evoke the greatest of earth memories, not those things which only satisfy curiosity, but those which uplift and inspire, and give us a vision of our own greatness; and the noblest of all Earth's memories is the august ritual of the ancient mysteries, where the mortal, amid scenes of unimaginable grandeur, was disrobed of his mortality and made of the company of the gods.[179]

In ancient times the task of the mysteries was to endow appropriately prepared individuals with wisdom. The task of people today is to work on spiritual-scientific findings, to 'carry them up in thought', to bring what they can learn on earth 'to the gods, for the times have changed'.[180] Only then can Michael live with the effects. 'Michael will be the real spiritual hero of freedom. He lets human beings act, but then receives the results of this human activity and bears them further into the cosmos in order to do with them in the cosmos what human beings can not yet do ... When, through reading the astral light, a human being is moved in freedom to do consciously or unconsciously one thing or another, then Michael bears what is earthly human deed out into the cosmos so that it becomes cosmic deed. He is concerned with effects, other spirits more with causes ... For this is what one learns to strive for more and more: to engage in contemplation as it were, in order to pierce through to the astral light, to see the secrets of existence, and then to come before Michael and receive his affirming gaze which says to one: That is right, that is just in the eyes of the powers who guide the cosmos.'[181]

Based on these facts, it is very evident that founding a new life of the mysteries will be no small undertaking. Even though this is the task of the Anthroposophical Society, we can only prepare for it. The decision as to what it will look like and what conditions will appertain to it, is made elsewhere!

Our starting point [in this book] was to ask how it is possible for a society like the Anthroposophical Society to come about in our materially oriented cultural environment. The answer could go like this: because at all times in human history knowledge has been preserved, through the working of the mysteries, of the divine origin of the world and the spiritual origin of humanity. Even after the withdrawal of the mysteries, the schools founded by them passed on enough of the genuine knowledge that by means of these traditional concepts at least an outline of understanding could be attained on earth. Through the Mystery of Golgotha, by those who felt connected with it, this outline of the spirit was then expanded and developed. This later brought these same individuals to the School of Michael where the urge arose for 'anthroposophy'. Through the study of anthroposophy on the earth, an awareness grew that the time had come to found the mysteries anew. Rudolf Steiner did all the preparatory work for this by secretly linking up in the first phase of the Anthroposophical Society's development with the Greek mysteries, the mysteries of the light, and renewing these by bringing [the idea of] development into the intellectual and spiritual life. He became a teacher of people. In the second phase of the Society's development he linked up with the Egyptian mysteries and their mysteries of space. He also renewed these by taking the spiritual life and making visible the forms that relate to it. Rudolf Steiner became the great example for a community who worked together with him to bring this magnificent work about. And finally, in the third phase of the Society's development, Steiner managed to rediscover the northern mysteries and the mysteries of the earth, in order to receive the impulse from them that is necessary to renew our whole culture and civilization. Those members who were in a position to contribute to this work became Rudolf Steiner's co-workers. The High School of Spiritual Science was intended to be a continuous source of renewal for all of anthroposophy. From there the impulses can come that are needed for the various specialist fields and the various institutions.

This whole movement serves the deeper goal of founding a new life of the mysteries. Then not only would the various formerly one-sided streams be here harmoniously united, not only would the dead and the unborn who are bound with Michael work together here, but people would also be aware here that we have obligations towards the Spirit and the spirits, and that only by working together with them might what is needed for the well-being of our modern culture then be realized.

Appendix
The Foundation Stone Meditation
(Version 1)*

Soul of Man!
Thou livest in the limbs
Which bear thee through the world of space
Into the spirit's ocean-being.
Practise spirit-recalling
In depths of soul,
Where in the wielding will
Of world-creating
Thine own I
Comes to being
Within God's I.
And thou wilt truly live
In the World-Being of Man.

For the Father-Spirit of the heights holds sway
In depths of worlds begetting being:
Seraphim, Cherubim, Thrones!
Let there ring out from the heights
What in the depths is echoed
Speaking:
Ex Deo nascimur.

The spirits of the elements hear it
In East, West, North, South:
May human beings hear it.

Soul of Man!
Thou livest in the beat of heart and lung
Which leads thee through the rhythm of time
Into the realm of thine own soul's feeling.
Practise spirit-awareness
In balance of the soul,
Where the surging deeds

---

* Translated by Michael Wilson. Taken from *The Foundation Stone: The Life, Nature and Cultivation of Anthroposophy*, Rudolf Steiner Press 1996.

Of the world's becoming
Thine own I
Unite
With the World-I.
And thou wilt truly feel
In the Soul-Weaving of Man.

For the Christ-Will in the encircling round holds sway
In the rhythms of the worlds, bestowing grace on the soul:
Kyriotetes, Dynamis, Exusiai,
Let there be fired from the East
What in the West is formed,
Speaking:
In Christo morimur.

The spirits of the elements hear it
In East, West, North, South:
May human beings hear it.

Soul of Man!
Thou livest in the resting head
Which from the grounds of eternity
Opens to thee the world-thoughts.
Practise spirit-beholding
In stillness of thought,
Where the eternal aims of Gods
World-Being's Light
On thine own I
Bestow
For thy free willing.
And thou wilt truly think
In the Spirit-Foundations of Man.

For the world-thoughts of the Spirit hold sway
In the being of worlds, craving for light:
Archai, Archangeloi, Angeloi!
Let there be prayed from the depths
What in the heights will be granted,

Speaking:
Per Spiritum Sanctum reviviscimus.

The spirits of the elements hear it
In East, West, North, South:
May human beings hear it.

At the turning of the time
The Spirit-Light of the world
Entered the stream of earthly being.
Darkness of night
Had held its sway,
Day-radiant light
Streamed into souls of men.
Light that gives warmth
To simple shepherds' hearts,
Light that enlightens
The wise heads of kings.

Light Divine
Christ-Sun!
Warm thou our hearts,
Enlighten thou our heads,

That good may become
What we from our hearts would found
What we from our heads would direct
In conscious
Willing.

(Version 2)[†]

Human Soul!
You live within the limbs
Which bear you through the world of space
Into the spirits' ocean-being.
Practice *spirit–recalling*
In depths of soul,
Where in the wielding
World-Creator-Being
Your own I
Comes into being
In the I of God;
And you will truly *live*
In human world-all being.

For the Father-Spirit of the heights holds sway
In depths of worlds begetting life.
Spirits of Strength:
Let ring forth from the heights
What in the depths is echoed,
Speaking:
Out of the Godhead we are born.

This is heard by the spirits of the elements
In east, west, north, south:
May human beings hear it!

Human soul!
You live within the beat of heart and lung
Which leads you through the rhythms of time
Into the feeling of your own soul-being.
Practice *spirit–sensing*
In balance of the soul,
Where the surging deeds
Of World-evolving
Unite your own I

[†] Translator unknown.

With the I of the World;
And you will truly *feel*
In human soul's creating.

For the Christ-will encircling us holds sway,
In world rhythms, bestowing grace upon souls,
Spirits of Light:
Let from the east be enkindled
What through the west takes on form,
Speaking:
In Christ, death becomes life.

This is heard by the spirits of the elements
In east, west, north, south:
May human beings hear it!

Human Soul!
You live within the resting head
Which from the grounds of eternity
Unlocks for you world-thoughts:
Practice *spirit–beholding*
In stillness of thought,
Where the gods' eternal aims
Bestow the light of cosmic being
On your own I
For free and active willing.
And you will truly *think*
In human spirit depths.

For the Spirit's world-thoughts hold sway
In cosmic being, imploring light.
Spirits of Soul:
Let from the depths be entreated
What in the heights will be heard,
Speaking:
In the spirit's cosmic thoughts the soul awakens.
This is heard by the spirits of the elements
In east, west, north, south:
May human beings hear it!

At the turning point of time
The Spirit-light of the world
Entered the stream of earth existence.
Darkness of night
Had ceased its reign;
Day-radiant light
Shone forth in human souls.
Light
That gives warmth
To simple shepherds' hearts;
Light
That enlightens
The wise heads of kings.

Light divine,
Christ-Sun,
Warm
Our hearts;
Enlighten
Our heads;
That good may become
What from our hearts
We are founding,
What from our heads
We direct,
With focused will.

NOTES

Works by Rudolf Steiner are quoted according to the Gesamtausgabe number (GA) of the Rudolf Steiner Verlag, Dornach, Switzerland. The title of each volume is given once, and thereafter only as a GA number. A list of GAs available in English translation is given on p. 170.

1 *Das menschliche Dilemma*, edited by Aurelio Peccei, Vienna and Munich 1979, page 11.
2 Op. cit., p. 52 and p. 68.
3 See the work by Sergei O. Prokofieff, *May Human Beings Hear it!* Sussex 2004, which was published after the completion of this book.
4 Berlin 1905.
5 F. W. J. Schelling, Die Welalter, 1811, I, in: M Schöter (edit.) *Schellings Werke*, Nachlassband, Munich 1946, p. 85 f.
6 After his discovery of the archetypal plant, Goethe also writes in a letter on 6 Sept 1787 *(Italian Journey)* of the ἑν καί παν which filled him with wonder.
7 J. W. Goethe, *Zur Morphologie*, 'Die Absicht eingeleitet', Hamburg edition, volume 13, Munich 1975, p. 55 f.
8 'Verfolg, Bedenken und Ergebung', op. cit., p. 31.
9 J. W. v. Goethe, *Zur Morphologie*, volume 1, supplement VIII, Frankfurt edition, volume 24, Frankfurt 1987, p. 504.
10 Letter of 13 February 1775.
11 J. G. Fichte, *Von den Pflichten der Gelehten*, edited by R. Lauth, Hamburg 1971, p. 34 f.
12 Op. cit., p. 97.
13 Op. cit., p. 36.
14 R. Steiner, *Mein Lebensgang*, GA 28, Chap III.
15 Op. cit., ebd.
16 At this point I do not want to go into Walter Johannes Steins 'conversation' with Steiner in The Hague, the content of which I consider to be largely misunderstood. For nowhere do we find in Steiner anything about a 'taking on' of Karl Julius Schröer's destiny, neither in *The Course of My Life* nor anywhere else in Steiner's works. On the contrary, wherever he mentions his Goethe task, he speaks expressly about it being apportioned to him by destiny!
17 *The Course of My Life*, chap. XII.
18 See F. Teichmann, *Aufersehung im Denken*, Stuttgart 1996.
19 Lecture on 24 April 1917 in *Bausteine zu einer Erkenntnis des Mysteriums von Golgatha*, GA 175.
20 *The Course of My Life*, chap. XXVI.
21 R. Steiner, lecture on 7 April 1922, in *Damit der Mensch ganz Mensch werde*, GA 82.

22 *The Course of My Life*, chap. XXIX.

23 R. Steiner, lecture on 23 June 1923, in *Die Geschichte und die Bedingungen der anthroposophischen Bewegung im Verhältnis zur Anthroposophischen Gesellschaft,* GA 258.

24 Op. cit., ebd.

25 Op. cit., ebd.

26 See the report on this lecture of 8 October 1902, in *Über Philosophie, Geschichte und Literature,* GA 258.

27 I. H. Fichte, *Grundzüge zum System der Philosophie,* volume 1, *Erkennen als Selbsterkennen*, Heidelberg 1833, p. 208.

28 Letter by R. Steiner to Hübbe-Schleiden, printed in *Beiträge zur Rudolf Steiner-Gesamtausgabe no. 79/80*, Easter 1983, p. 33 f.

29 R. Steiner, lecture on 6 February 1923, in *Anthroposophische Gemeinshafts-bildurng,* GA 257.

30 R. Steiner, lecture on 11 June 1923, GA 258.

31 R. Steiner, lecture on 6 February 1923, GA 257.

32 Currently in *Zur Geschichte und aus den Inhalten der ersten Abteilung der Esoterischen Schule,* GA 264, and *Aus den Inhalten der esoterischen Stunden,* GA 266, volume 1-3.

33 R. Steiner, lecture on 15 December 1919, in *Die Sendung Michaels,* GA 194.

34 Op. cit.,

35 R. Steiner, lecture on 22 April 1917, in GA 175.

36 Op. cit.,

37 R. Steiner, lecture on 3 April 1917, in GA 175.

38 Translated by W. U. Klünker, Stuttgart 1987.

39 Op. cit.

40 Quoted from H. Ehret, *I. H. Fichte*, Stuttgart 1986, p. 73.

41 In *Kürschners Deutsche Nationalliterature, Goethes Werke,* part 33, Scientific Writings, Berlin and Stuttgart, 1884.

42 See *The Course of My Life*, Chap. XII.

43 See R. Steiner, lecture on 16 September 1924, in *Karmic Relationships*, Volume IV, GA 238.

44 See page 21.

45 R. Steiner, in the lecture of 16 October 1918, in *Der Tod als Lebenswandlung,* GA 182.

46 R. Steiner, lecture on 6 February 1923, in GA 257.

47 Op. cit.

48 Op. cit.

49 R. Steiner, letter of 25 November 1905, in *Rudolf Steiner/Marie von Sivers: Briefwechsel und Dokumente 1901-1925,* GA 262.

50 From R. Steiner's report on the congress in *Luzifer-Gnosis* no. 37, in *Bilder okkulter Siegel und Säulen*, GA 284.

51 Op. cit.

52 Op. cit.

53 Op. cit.
54 Op. cit.
55 Lecture on 19 May 1907, in GA 284.
56 Op. cit.
57 End of lecture on 21 May 1907, in GA 284.
58 See page 36.
59 See G. Kačer-Bock, *Die Mysteriendramen im Lebensgang Rudolf Steiners*, Stuttgart 1995.
60 From a description by Max Gümbel-Seiling on 5 April 1909, in GA 284.
61 GA 126.
62 Hölderlin's entry in Hegel's album was written on 12 February 1791 with a quote from Goethe's *Iphigenie*. The ἑν καί παν is written afterwards in Hegel's hand. See Hölderlin, *Zum 200. Geburtstag*, exhibition catalogue by W. Volke, Munich 1970, p. 116.
63 From the dedication address on 15 October 1911, GA 284.
64 Op. cit.
65 The following entries are in the minute book of the Building Group of the Stuttgart Anthroposophists, 22 December 1910: M. 5000 subsequently approved to S (Schmid-Curtius) for everything necessary for the columns in the lower floor. On 1 September 1911, 'Herr del Monte asked to contact Frl. Rettich to give her the final sketches for the 'seals', M 2000 budgeted for this purpose.
66 See M. Steiner, *Ein durch Rudolf Steiner gegebener Zukunftsimpulse und was zunächst daraus geworden ist* (An impulse for the future given by Rudolf Steiner, and what has come of it), Dornach 1947.
67 See the unpublished work by Benzinger on *Bauerlebnisse und Anderes*. In more detail see also: Sonja Ohlenschläger, *Rudolf Steiner, das architektonische Werk*, Petersberg 1999, p. 76.
68 This and following quotes from *Das Goetheanum in seinen zehn Jahren. Sieben Aufsätze aus dem Jahr 1923*, in *Der Goetheanumgedanke inmitten der Kulturkrisis der Gegenwart*, GA 36.
69 *Anweisungen für eine esoterische Schulung*, GA 245, now also in *Mantrische Sprüche*, GA 268.
70 Lecture on 12 December 1911 at the first general meeting of the Johannes-Bau Verein.
71 Article of 4 February 1923, in GA 36.
72 Letter of 25 November 1905 to Marie von Sivers, in GA 262.
73 *The Course of My Life*, chap. XXXVI.
74 *Zur Geschichte und zu den Inhalten der erkenntniskultischen Abteilung der Esoterischen Schule*, GA 265.
75 From 16 December 1911, in GA 265.
76 From the first article in *Das Goetheanum in seinen zehn Jahren*, GA 36.
77 *The Course of My Life*, Chap XXXVI.
78 GA 265, Notes from the lesson in Berlin on 16 December 1911.
79 See F. Teichmann, *Die Ägyptischen Mysterien*, Stuttgart 1999. *The Sacred Mysteries of Egypt*, Edinburgh 2016.

80 Op. cit., p. 212 ff.
81 E. Schuré, *Das heilige Drama von Eleusis* (The Sacred Drama of Eleusis), Dornach 1939, p. 17.
82 On 19 May 1907, in GA 284.
83 See F. Teichmann, *Die ägyptischen Mysterien,* Stuttgart 1999, p. 17. See note 79.
84 See the beautiful presentation of these transformations in: J W Rohen, *Morphologie des menschlichen Organismus,* Stuttgart 2000.
85 For example, see lectures by Steiner on 20 July 1923 in *Drei Perspektiven der Anthroposophie,* GA 225; on 21 November 1919 in GA 194; on 29 January 1918 in *Erdensterben und Weltenleben,* GA 181, and in many other places.
86 From the fifth article in *Das Goetheanum in seinen zehn Jahren,* on 18 February 1923, GA 36.
87 *Zeitgeschichtliche Betrachtungen. Das Karma der Unwahrhaftigkeit—Part 1,* GA 173, lecture on 21 December 1916.
88 In GA 284.
89 See Marie Steiner's *Ein durch Rudolf Steiner gegebener Zukunftsimpuls und was zunächst daraus geworden ist,* Dornach 1947.
90 Lecture on 21 December 1917, in *Geschichtlich Notwendigkeit und Freiheit,* GA 179.
91 Lecture on 29 December 1917, in *Mysterienwahrheiten und Weihnachtsimpulse,* GA 180.
92 See page 46 and frontispiece.
93 Lecture on 29 December 1918, in *Wie kann die Menschheit den Christus wiederfinden?,* GA 187.
94 Lecture on 27 April, in *Esoterische Betrachtungen karmischer Zusammenhänge,* Volume V, GA 239.
95 Lecture on 6 January 1918, in GA 180.
96 See *Die Grundimpulse des weltgeschichtlichen Werdens der Menschheit,* GA 216, particularly lecture on 24 September 1922.
97 Lecture on 13 February 1923, in GA 257.
98 Lecture on 24 December 1923, in *Die Weihnachtstagung zur Begündung der Allgemeinen Anthroposophischen Gesellschaft,* GA 260.
99 *Gegenwartiges Geistesleben und Erziehung,* GA 307.
100 See F. Teichmann, *Die Megalithkultur,* Stuttgart 1997, and R Steiner, lecture on 10 Sept. 1923, in *Initiationwissenschaft und Sternenerkenntnis,* GA 228.
101 Lecture on 10 September 1923, GA 228.
102 Lecture on 9 September 1923, now in *Initiationserkenntnis,* GA 227.
103 Lecture on 14 Semptember 1923, in GA 228.
104 Lecture on 9 September 1923, in GA 227.
105 On 9 September 1923 in: *Rudolf Steiner und die Zivilisationsaufgaben der Anthroposophie,* Dornach 1943.
106 See Rudolf Steiner's seal for his mystery drama *Der Hüter der Schwelle.* (See frontispiece.)
107 See Zeylmans van Emmichoven, *Wer war Ita Wegman,* volume I, Heidelberg, 1990, p. 146.

108 Lecture on 9 September 1923, in GA 227.
109 *Das Miterleben des Jahreslaufes in vier kosmischen Imaginationen,* GA 229.
110 Lecture on 12 October 1923, in GA 229.
111 Lecture on 9 September 1923, in GA 227.
112 Lecture on 14 September 1923, in GA 228.
113 Lecture on 30 September 1923, in *Der Jahreslauf als Atmungsvorgang der Erde,* GA 223.
114 Letter of 30 August 1923, in *Rudolf Steiner/Edith Maryon: Briefwechsel,* GA 263/1.
115 With the exception of the laying of the foundation stone of the first Goetheanum.
116 Lecture on 12 August 1923, in GA 307.
117 This and the following quotes from the lecture on 25 December 1923, in GA 260.
118 GA 233a.
119 On 31 August 1923, now in GA 227.
120 Lecture on 9 September 1923, now in GA 227, p. 359.
121 Lecture on 14 September 1923, in GA 228.
122 Lecture on 23 February 1924, in *Esoterische Betrachtungen karmischer Zusammenhänge, (Karmic Relationships) Vol. 1.* GA 235.
123 Beginning of the first letter to members on 20 January 1924, in *Die Konstitution...,* GA 260a.
124 See Zeylmans van Emmichoven, *Wer war Ita Wegman,* Vol 1.
125 In GA 228.
126 Now in GA 227.
127 Final address in Penmaenmawr, printed in: *Rudolf Steiner und die Zivilisationsaufgaben der Anthroposophie,* Dornach 1943, p. 155. See *Rudolf Steiner Speaks to the British,* London 1998.
128 J. W. von Goethe, *Wilhelm Meister,* Book 1, Chap. 17.
129 See for example F. Teichmann, *Auferstehung im Denken,* Stuttgart 1996.
130 Published in 1886, GA 2.
131 *The Course of My Life,* Chapter XII.
132 Op. cit.,
133 J. W. v. Goethe, Conversation on 1 October 1828.
134 *The Course of My Life,* Chapter XII.
135 Op. cit., end of Chapter XIII.
136 Op. cit., end of Chapter XII.
137 Op. cit., Chapter XXX.
138 Printed today in *Luzifer-Gnosis,* GA 34.
139 Oskar Schmiedel, in *Erinnerungen an Rudolf Steiner* (Memories of Rudolf Steiner), published by E Beltle, Stuttgart 2001, p. 99.
140 Op. cit., p. 96/97.
141 Op. cit., p. 84.

142 Op. cit., p. 81.

143 See *Entwürfe, Fragmente und Paralipomena zu den vier Mysteriendramen* (Designs, fragments and paralipomena for the four Mystery Dramas), GA 44.

144 R. Steiner, lecture on 14 September 1924, in GA 238.

145 R. Steiner, lecture on 1 January 1924, in GA 233a.

146 R. Steiner, lecture on 9 September 1924, in GA 227.

147 See the Arnheim lecture on 18-20 July 1924 in *Karmic Relationships*, Volume VI, GA 240.

148 R. Steiner, lecture on 18 July 1924, in GA 240.

149 R. Steiner, lecture on 14 September 1924, in GA 238.

150 Op. cit., page 92.

151 R. Steiner, lecture on 12 January 1919, in *Der Goetheanismus, ein Umwandlungsimpuls und Auferstehungsgedanke* (Goetheanism: an impulse for transformation and a concept of resurrection), GA 188.

152 All quotes from the same lecture on 12 January 1919.

153 R. Steiner, lecture on 11 October 1913, in *Okkulte Untersuchungen über das Leben zwischen Tod und neuer Geburt* (Occult research into the life between death and a new birth), GA 140.

154 R. Steiner, lecture on 21 September 1911, in *Das esoterische Christentum* (Esoteric Christianity), GA 130.

155 R. Steiner, GA 233a.

156 See lecture on 15 December 1919, in GA 194.

157 R. Steiner, lecture on 27 December 1918, in GA 187.

158 R. Steiner, lecture on 26 September 1909, in *Gospel of St Luke*, GA 114.

159 For a comparison of these three types of culture, see F. Teichmann, *Der Mensch und sein Tempel: Megalithkultur* (Man and his temple: megalithic culture), Stuttgart 1999.

160 See Ignaz von Born, 'Über die Mysterien der Ägyptier', in *Journal für Freimaurer,* Vol. 1, Vienna 1784, p. 17-132.

161 F. W. J. Schelling, Berlin, 1802.

162 Op. cit., p. 34.

163 F .W. J. Schelling, in *Urfassung der Philosophie der Offenbarung* (Original draft of the philosophy of manifestation), 2 vols. edited by Walter E. Ehrhardt, Hamburg 1992, Vol. 1, p. 197.

164 Lecture on 16 September 1924, in GA 240.

165 Lecture on 12 September 1924, in GA 240.

166 Lecture on 16 September 1924, in GA 240.

167 The bridge to the Michael-being is established by Tycho de Brahe = Julian the Apostate, which we do not need to look into here.

168 See Plato, *Republic*, Book 7.

169 Lecture on 30 January 1923, in GA 257. This was also quoted in another context in Chapter 3.

170 Lecture on 16 October 1918, in GA 182.

171 Origen, *Vier Bücher von den Prinzipien* (Four books on the principles), edited

and translated by G. Görgemanns and H. Karpp, Darmstadt 1967, p. 447.

172 Lecture on 1 January 1924, *World History in the Light of Anthroposophy,* GA 233.

173 Lecture on 20 April 1924, in GA 233 a.

174 Lecture on 22 April 1924, in GA 233 a.

175 Op. cit.,

176 Lecture on 13 January 1924, in GA 233 a.

177 Lecture on 19 December 1912, in *Das Leben zwischen dem Tode und der neuen Geburt im Verhältnis zu den kosmischen Tatsachen* (Life between death and a new birth in relation to cosmic facts), GA 141.

178 Lecture of 18 July 1924, in GA 240.

179 G.W. Russell ['A.E.'], *The Candle of Vision,* end of chapter on 'The Memoryof the Earth'.

180 Lecture on 13 January 1924, in GA 233 a.

181 Op. cit.

Illustrations

Frontispiece: by kind permission of Rudolf Steiner Nachlassverwaltung.
Illus. 3 and 14: from GA 284, by kind permission of Rudolf Steiner Nachlassverwaltung.
Illus. 8: from a Greek manuscript in the Biblioteca Nazionale Marciano, Venice.
Illus. 19-22: photos by O. Rietmann, by kind permission of Verlag am Goetheanum.
Illus. 30-31: Calendar 1912/13, by kind permission of Rudolf Steiner Nachlassverwaltung.
Illus. 52: 'Druidenstein', by kind permission of Rudolf Steiner Nachlassverwaltung.
Illus. 60: Rudolf Steiner, photo by Rietmann, by kind permission of Verlag am Goetheanum.

Bibliography of Works by Rudolf Steiner

The following volumes are cited in this book. Where relevant, published editions of equivalent English translations are provided.

RSP = Rudolf Steiner Press, UK
AP / SB = Anthroposophic Press / SteinerBooks, USA

2 *Goethe's Theory of Knowledge*, SB

28 *Autobiography*, SB

34 *Lucifer-Gnosis; Grundlegende Aufsätze zur Anthroposophie und Berichte aus den Zeitschriften 'Luzifer' und 'Lucifer – Gnosis' 1903 – 1908*

36 *Der Goetheanumgedanke inmitten der Kulturkrisis der Gegenwart: Gesammelte Aufsätze aus der Wochenschrift 'Das Goetheanum' 1921–1925*

44 *Entwürfe, Fragmente und Paralipomena zu den vier Mysteriendramen*

82 *Damit der Mensch ganz Mensch werde*

114 *According to Luke*, SB

126 *Occult History*, RSP

130 *Esoteric Christianity and the Mystery of Christian Rosenkreutz*, RSP

140 *Okkulte Untersuchungen über das Leben zwischen Tod und neuer Geburt. Die lebendige Wechselwirkung zwischen Leben und Tod*

141 *Life Between Death and Rebirth*, AP

173 *Karma of Untruthfulness*, Vol 1, RSP

175 *Building Stones for an Understanding of the Mystery of Golgotha*, RSP

179 *Influence of the Dead on Destiny*, SB

180 *Mysterienwahrheiten und Weihnachtsimpulse. Alte Mythen und ihre Bedeutung. Geistige Wesen und Ihre Wirkung*, Band IV

181 *Dying Earth and Living Cosmos*, RSP

182 *Death as Metamorphosis of Life*, SB

187 *How can Mankind find the Christ*, AP

188 *Der Goetheanismus, ein Umwandlungsimpuls und Auferstehungsgedanke. Menschenwissenschaft und Sozialwissenschaft*

194 *Michael's Mission*, SB

216 *Die Grundimpulse des weltgeschlichtlichen Werdens der Menschheit*

223 *Anthroposophy and the Human Gemüt*, AP

225 *Drei Perspektiven der Anthroposophie. Kulturphänomene, geisteswissenschaftlich betrachtet*

227 *Evolution of Consciousness*, RSP

228 *Initiation Science*, RSP
229 *Das Miterleben des Jahreslaufes in vier kosmischen Imaginationen*
233 *World History and the Mysteries*, RSP
233a *Rosicrucianism and Modern Initation*, RSP
235 *Karmic Relationships*, Vol I, RSP
238 *Karmic Relationships*, Vol, IV, RSP
239 *Karmic Relationships*, Vol VII, RSP
240 *Karmic Relationships*, Vol VIII, RSP
245 *Guidance in Esoteric Training*, RSP
257 *Awakening to Community*, AP
258 *Life, Nature and Cultivation of Anthroposophy*, RSP
260 *The Christmas Conference for the Foundation of the General Anthroposophical Society*, AP/RSP
260a *Anthroposophical Leading Thoughts*, RSP
262 *Letters and Documents*, RSP
263/1 *Rudolf Steiner - Edith Maryon: Briefwechsel. Briefe - Sprüche - Skizzen, 1912-1924*
264 *From the History and Contents of the First Section of the Esoteric School 1904-1914*, SB
265 *Freemasonry and Ritual Work*, SB
266 *Esoteric Lessons, Vols. 1-3*, SB
268 *Mantric Sayings, Meditations 1903 – 1925, Soul exercises, 1903-1925*, SB
284 *Rosicrucianism Renewed*, SB
307 *A Modern Art of Education*, RSP

All English-language titles are available via Rudolf Steiner Press, UK (www.rudolfsteinerpress.com) or SteinerBooks, USA (www.steinerbooks.org)